journey of an art quilter

CREATIVE STRATEGIES AND TECHNIQUES

BARBARA OLSON

First U.S. edition published in 2004

© 2004 Barbara Olson

Publisher and chief editor: Linda C. Teufel
Graphic design: Kimberly Koloski
Photography: Larry Friar (except where noted)
Editors: Linda Wolf Jackson, Pat Radloff,
Rebecca Frazier, Carol Powalisz

Publisher's Cataloging in Publication Data
Olson, Barbara
Journey of an Art Quilter:
Creative Strategies & Techniques
Quilting
Sewing
I. Title

Library of Congress Catalog Card Number:
2003111261

ISBN# 0-9641201-8-6

9 8 7 6 5 4 3 2 1

Printed in Thailand

Dragon Threads
490 Tucker Drive
Worthington, OH 43085
www.dragonthreads.com

dedication

This book is dedicated to all the creative quilters that have touched my life and inspired me to share my journey in this book.

To my precious mother whose love of life and joyful presence guided me through life and is still guiding me from above.

contents

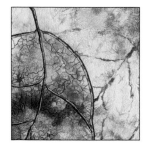

appreciation

I give my love and thanks to my husband Larry who made my exploration of my creative talents possible. His emotional and financial base supported me through this ongoing artistic journey. When his engineering mind did not understand, his heart took over and gave me unfailing support.

Undying gratitude to my daughter Jennifer who is my spiritual resource, my inspiration, and my friend. Jennifer's insight, that my passion for creating quilts is the key to my life's purpose, helped give me the confidence to develop quilting as a career. Her belief that I must share these quilts and their creation is an ever-present reminder to carry on.

Words cannot express my gratitude to my talented and cherished friend Linda Wolf Jackson for her boundless support. The generous gift of her time, her editorial skills and her ability to guide my creative vision has made this book a possibility for me.

My thanks goes to Dragon Threads and Linda Teufel, my superb editor, who understood and supported my vision for a unique art quilt book and guided it into being. I give my gratitude for her communication skills and for taking me by the hand and guiding me through the process. I am thankful for the friendship that has developed and our common vision for this publication. Thank you to the talented graphic designer, Kimberly Koloski, for presenting my images and words in a beautiful energy-filled format. Thanks to Larry Friar for his beautiful photography for this book.

Appreciation goes to my students who were willing to share their wonderfully unique art quilts in this book. Their creative spirit is a constant inspiration. Thank you to all the collectors of my work who generously shared their quilts with us for the photo shoot.

My quilting family—Marjo Nash, Marj Taylor and Helen Eckert (who is expressing her creative spirit from above)—thank you for your ongoing support and love. Last but not least, thanks to my sons Scott and Darryl, who have lived with my constant quilting work and whose requests were most often met with the response, "Let me finish one last stitch." Their patience and love helped support this exciting adventure.

I would like to express my gratitude to all the vendors who provided wonderful products to develop quilts for this book.

introduction

This book has come into being because I feel so passionately about the importance of each and everyone of us accessing our unique visions and manifesting them in some form. There are many wonderful images dancing around in the creative minds of quilters and many unique quilts waiting to be born. It is my hope that the ideas, techniques and journey that I share in this book will have an influence in many dazzling quilts being created.

As I travel through the country presenting workshops and lectures, I have the privilege of meeting many informed and innovative quilters. These quilters have a willingness to learn, to experience new ways of thinking and creating. Whether new to quilting or a seasoned professional, they are looking for not only cutting-edge techniques but motivation and inspiration. It is my goal to meet all these needs in this bold, evolutionary book in which my quilts provide a backdrop for personal development tools, concise information and step-by-step techniques.

As I share my journey, most of you will be able to relate to my love of quilting, and to the joy of creating. The journey from quilter to quilt artist is a journey many of

Kiss of the Creative Fire, 2000. 70" × 60"
Collection of Salley Davey, Berkeley, CA

you are on or are going to begin. For those of you new to exploring innovative quilt-making, this book can be used as an entire learning experience from beginning to end. You will start with pivotal exercises on understanding and using innate creative styles and then explore ten techniques to help construct your unique images. For the adventuresome spirit, this book is filled with creative ideas and challenging possibilities. It can also be used as a resource for problem solving or learning new techniques. It will challenge you, inspire you, and dare you to play.

The ideas and quilts presented in *Journey of an Art Quilter* are the accumulation of seventeen years of quilting and personal development. I have drawn on my creative experiences in the studio, my willingness to design outside the lines and make mistakes (which led to creating award-winning quilts) and from ten years of presenting workshops. I have also shared the techniques I have developed and problem solving methods. My lack of formal art education has not stopped me from presenting wonderfully unique fiber pieces to the world nor should anyone else be stopped from doing the same because they lack formal art training. Let intuition, your willing spirit and the pure joy of creating be your guide as you journey through this book.

Release the light and energy from matter in your images.

the journey begins

My journey into the world of quilting began when I saw an ad in an adult education brochure for an eight-week basic quilting class. "That might be fun," I thought, so I registered for it. Little did I know what a powerful impact this action would have on my life in the future.

My mother, who was an excellent seamstress, taught me to sew at a young age. I began making doll clothes and then, as my skills improved, garments. Quilting was not a part of my experience growing up or as a young adult, nor was art or any art training. Color, especially playing with bright, brilliant colors, always fascinated me. I used it in whatever I did, including interior decorating and many different types of crafts, but my passion wasn't really ignited until I combined my love of color and sewing into my first quilt.

As I sat in the classroom during that first night of the basic quilting class and looked at the teacher's beautiful sampler quilts, listened to her talk about fabric, and watched her present the patterns we were to use, I was hooked. It felt like I had come home. This way of creating totally engaged my energy. I was unaware of it at the time, but I had always been attracted to quilt designs. When my mother recently gave me some of my old junior high and high school notebooks, I was amazed to find that, along with boys' names, I had doodled hundreds of quilting blocks, usually Mariner's Compass or other blocks with a center-oriented design. Again, I had no exposure to quilting blocks or patterns, but apparently they were part of the internal program that came with me into this world. I have since learned, through research and study, that everything about me—my brain type, my personality, and my way of moving through the world—all fit perfectly with the creative world of quilting. It took me 38 years to connect my creativity to the world of quilting, but when I finally did, my unique journey began.

In the pages that follow, I will recount my journey and introduce you to the tools and techniques that helped me evolve my work from traditional quilting to art quilting. This journey not only allowed me to physically express the unique images in my mind, but also provided me opportunities to turn my creativity and passion into a career of teaching, lecturing and writing, which I absolutely love. The journey transformed not only my creative life, but also my personal life.

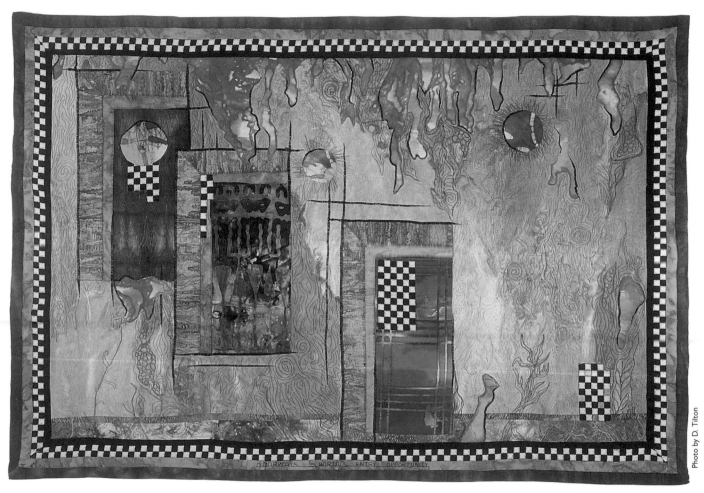

Doctor's note illegible

Doorways, 2002. 36" x 24"
Collection of Dionne Hersh-Matthies and Carol Beck.

The dignity of my life lies in living my own unique story.

an artist emerges

Most people who meet me would describe me as laid-back, quiet and traditional. It would never enter most people's minds to call me a rebel or think of me as someone who breaks the rules. My children laugh when I talk about being a rule-breaker. But when you look at my quilts, they are anything but traditional and quiet and they do indeed break the rules. I express my flamboyance through my quilts; in them I can convey my love of color. The unique, joyful energy that I have to offer is displayed for the entire world to see in my art quilts.

believe that if given the opportunity and freedom, many people would reveal their own hidden, beautiful, exciting energy in quilts. To do so, people need a safe environment in which to learn—an environment that fellow quilters certainly provide. Also needed are a nurturing teacher or mentor and a willing spirit; with these things, anyone's energy will shine through. There are many wonderful teachers, mentors and workshops out there. Take advantage of them—and with a willingness to try, a willingness to make mistakes (I have made multitudes), your creative energies will start to flow. Along my journey, I found a safe place to learn, I found excellent teachers and mentors and I was willing to try new things without fear of mistakes. Creative, supportive friends are one of the

I flew—or fell—out of the quilting nest…

greatest gifts that I have been given on this journey. Great teachers (both local and national) have given me the tools I needed—not just the quilting techniques, which formed the basis of my evolution, but also the creative support and inspiration.

In the basic quilting class where I began my journey, we were to make a nine-block sampler quilt. I was a good student and followed the rules—that was, until the last block when I just couldn't stand it any more and decided to change the setting of the block. It was not a successful design alteration, but I did it anyway. This was a behavior pattern that would continue through each class in which I participated over the years. As in the first class, the teachers would try to direct me, but usually ended up just shaking their heads and leaving me to my own devices.

inspiration & motivation

- The framework that quilt blocks provide is a safe place to explore the creative process.

- Experiment and break the rules within the safety of the framework.

- Extend outside the framework and eventually the framework no longer exists.

In retrospect, one of the reasons I was attracted to quilting was because of the framework it provided for the creative process. In my other art experiences, when given a blank canvas to create with, I got lost in all the possibilities and ended up producing a hodgepodge of unrelated images and symbols. Quilting patterns gave me a safe base to start from, but then I always had to add more lines, turn things around, and change the size or shape of the block. When it came to adding color, if the teacher called for three colors, I brought six. If the quilt needed a red fabric, I would use ten reds. Whatever the color, I was driven to use a wider variety within the color range—but even with all the experimenting and rule breaking, I still had the safety of the framework. I think many quilters, consciously or unconsciously, are attracted to the safety that the framework of quilting provides.

As my creative processes extended outside the framework, the framework eventually no longer existed. I flew, or fell, out of the quilting nest (most people are convinced that it was the latter when they look at my work) and began to create my original designs.

Sampler Quilt, 1986. 52" x 52"
Breaking the rules: I changed the setting of one block. See first row, second block from left. It was not a very successful design alteration, but I did it anyway.

The transformation from quilter to quilt artist, from blocks to original design, does not happen at the same rate or in the same way for everyone. For me, it was an educational and experimental

Plaid Vibrations, 1992. 24" x 30"

process that took place over six years. It was six years before I began to take myself seriously and really considered the possibility that I might have talent. It was six years of taking every class that I could, locally and regionally. I was blessed to belong to two local quilt guilds that valued education and offered workshops from many nationally recognized teachers and quilt artists.

My exposure to these teachers was a real catalyst to helping me leave the framework behind.

I was helped along the path to innovation by my willing spirit and an inborn desire to change and to try new things. A little ignorance also helped. I did not know all the rules of design or of the art world, so I had no fear when it came to thinking that I could create original artwork. A world of possibilities opened up to me when I came to the point where I was willing to leave behind the belief that every quilt I created had to have a purpose and a place. This was a hard belief to get past because I was raised in the world of practicality. I was taught to put food on the table or engage in things that had a utilitarian purpose. Sewing and quilting were acceptable because they produced an everyday useful product. Art, on the other hand, was considered frivolous. Spending money on such a foolish venture such as creating art quilts would have been unacceptable, but I persevered. I had already passed the point of no return. My desire and faith were in place and I was sure that I was on the right path, despite the fact my actions seemed contrary to the values in my background. It was a major revelation for me to create a quilt with no particular purpose in mind—doing so has allowed me to do what I do today. Without releasing my beliefs about purpose and practicality, I would not have created my award-winning art quilts, I would not be an international teacher and lecturer, and I would not be writing this book.

The first award I ever won for a quilt in an art category was at a county fair. This was at the beginning of my experimentation with art quilting. The quilt I entered won first place. My entry in this contest came about due to the particular way I have of approaching the world. I look at what other people do, and naïvely believe I can do it too, maybe even do it better, and then I take action. A belief without action is only wishful thinking. As I viewed the quilts at the art competition the prior year, I turned to comment about the pieces to a friend and said, "I can do this. I will have a piece in this show next year." The piece that won the award was *Plaid Vibrations*, a simple piece with little quilting that was fun to create. With this win, a thought began to form in the deep recesses of my mind, "Maybe I do have talent."

At this point, I was still pretty unaware of the impact that quilting was going to have on my entire life. I lived in the real world. I had a family that I adored and I was busy with all that goes along with having three children. I loved taking care of my home and creating a nur-

Maybe I do have talent…

- Leave behind the belief that every quilt you create has to have a purpose and a place and the world of possibilities will open up for you.
- If you think you would like to enter a quilt in a contest, the county fairs and local shows are a good place to start.

inspiration & motivation

turing environment. I also worked full time as the comptroller and interior designer for my husband's architectural/engineering firm. Where was I going to find the time to practice, to develop my skills? The thought of creating my own style hadn't even entered into my mind.

Village Sunrise, 1993. 64" x 64"
Private collection.

Reading books was good, but listening to tapes was even better because I could quilt while I listened.

I was trying to find out what my talent was and how to express my creativity. I wondered where I would find the information and tools I needed to do so. With so many books available on the subjects of finding your talent and accessing your creativity, it was hard to decide which were the best and where to start. Even with all these questions, I plunged ahead, reading and listening to everything I came across. Reading books on the subjects was good, but listening to books on tapes was even better because I could quilt while I listened. At that time, I had to special order many of my books and tapes (see resource list). Now most of these are available at the big bookstores or on the Internet.

I'm the type of person who has to confirm an idea from many different sources before I will take it seriously. This compulsion to verify has really helped me pinpoint some of the most useful tools for thinking creatively. The first tool that seemed to be prevalent throughout most of the material I encountered was meditation. Meditation is not necessarily the kind that many of us picture, i.e., sitting with legs crossed in the lotus position and chanting. Meditation can just involve sitting quietly and slowing down the input and programs always running in the mind. Our minds get so full of thoughts, memories, plans, and fears that we have few attention bytes (a computer analogy) available to deal with the here and now.

When sitting down to create, if you have even a little of your focus going to what happened yesterday, what problems you have or hurts you endured, or what you need to do tomorrow, then you are not fully present to the task at hand. We often miss seeing and doing so much because our brains are already full.

Imagine what it would be like to be able to clear your mind, restore your spirit and then step out into the world. Everything seems brighter; you are able to experience your environment at a heightened level. You are able to respond to people, places, and things with a greater attention. Some of the frayed nerves are healed and research has shown that meditation can also help the body heal as well. This is a win-win process. Meditation is one of the greatest gifts that you can give yourself. Your work will improve when you start doing it on a regular basis. With a more peaceful way of moving through your world, you will impact those around you in a positive way.

Using your brain is the slowest way to create. Using your intuition and feelings is the quickest way to create unique images.

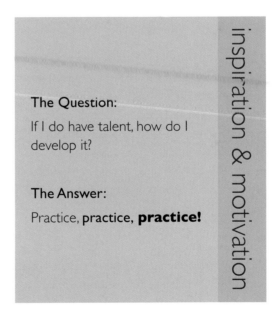

The Question:

If I do have talent, how do I develop it?

The Answer:

Practice, practice, **practice!**

inspiration & motivation

Meditating for 20 minutes a day is one of the greatest gifts that you can give yourself and your work.

As you begin each creative session, close your eyes, take three deep breaths, quiet your brain, and center yourself. Allow your creative energy to begin to flow.

Quieting the mind seemed impossible for me at first. My thoughts rolled around like a BB in a boxcar, but then I found that audiotapes were an excellent way to help quiet the mind. A valuable one that helped take me into a quiet, meditative state is *Drawing on the Light From Within* by Dr. Judith Cornell. It is a companion to her book of the same name, which was also extremely helpful. This tape uses imagery of light flowing through the body to help the listener relax and let go. It just takes 20 minutes a day to benefit from this type of meditation.

After I had been meditating for a while, friends and family whom I had not seen in months commented that I seemed like a different person. My way of interacting with them and those around me was much more peaceful and easy. The benefits that I realize from this process greatly outweigh the time I invest in it.

The first quilt I made that came directly out of the meditation process was *Village Sunrise* (p. 22). I did a meditation in which I envisioned a quilt filled with light right before I pulled the fabric and attended a workshop with Sharon Craig. The workshop involved playing with color and dimension using triangles, and during the course of the workshop, the central image of a teepee on sunlit wheat fields evolved. I encourage you to try this technique of getting your brain out of the way. If you do not have time for a full meditation, at least pause every time before you begin to work on a quilt. Though *Village Sunrise* was the first quilt I created as a result of meditation, there are many more. I have already given some form, while others are still in the drawing and idea stages.

Log Cabin Star, 1993. 30" x 30"

Sea of Fish, 1992. 28" x 28"

Yellow Diamonds, 1991. 42" x 42"

East Meets West, 1994. 60" x 60"
(Pattern from the book *East Quilts West* by Kumiko Sudo)

the light goes on

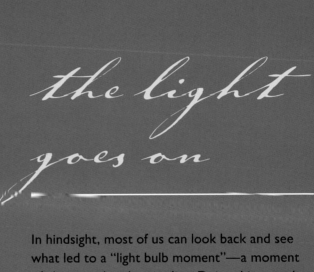

In hindsight, most of us can look back and see what led to a "light bulb moment"—a moment of clarity and understanding. Doing things such as taking classes, studying, experimenting with fabric, color and design, and having a willing spirit, all help lead us to these moments of understanding our unique creative style. For me, these "light bulb moments" are true revelations.

The catalyst for my understanding was one particular workshop I attended. It was a four-day workshop taught by a magnificent international quilt teacher and artist. When I looked at some of the quilts by this teacher, I was brought to tears because they were so wonderful. As I sat in her classroom, I gave thanks to the universe for the opportunity I saw before me. However, this workshop also presented me with some major challenges—I was unprepared for the feelings of creative and emotional torture that this workshop stirred up inside me. Still wondering if I really had any talent, I thought I should just give up. I had experienced some of these feelings in other quilt art workshops that I attended, but in this instance, these emotions were much more intense. I just did not get it; I did not connect with the

Asking the question "What if?"

process, which was to create a framework first and then fill it in. The teacher and the instruction were excellent, so what was wrong with me?

The four small blocks that I created in the four-day workshop sat in a drawer for a few weeks while I licked my wounds and began to heal. One day I got brave and put them up on the design wall. Still, nothing engaged my energy. The blocks just didn't speak to me.

The blocks hung on my design wall another few weeks. Friends came and went and made suggestions and comments. I tried a vertical setting. I tried different sashing fabrics for the framework—a framework I was trying to create after the fact, not before the fact as instructed. I even considered cutting up the blocks and adding more strips like the teacher suggested.

Then came the day when I walked into the studio (a small bedroom that I had commandeered) and asked myself, "What if I set the four blocks together to form a center mandala?" I tried it and when I viewed the blocks in this setting, it felt like an explosion of energy shot through me and I was connected to the design.

inspiration & motivation

Light bulb moments are usually the culmination of a learning process and then getting the brain out of the way.

It felt like an explosion of energy shot through me and I was connected to the design.

Why did the blocks now engage me? Why did I now see the possibilities and feel the energy begin to flow? Have you considered why your energy is engaged by a specific design style?

I did not know the answers to these questions at the time, so I began to look for the answers. I read and listened to books on tape, such as Howard Gardner's *Frames of Mind*, Robert J. Sternberg's *Handbook of Creativity*, Tony Robbins's programs on neuro-linguistic programming and Jonathan P. Niednagel's *Brain Typing*. These are just a few of the books available on the young science of understanding the brain and our innate ways of creating (see resource list). These books are about how contemporary brain researchers have found some basic types of programs and intelligences (or "software," to use a computer term) that we come into this world with, and from where our uniqueness emerges. These sources go on

to describe the intelligences in detail, which helped me begin to discern my own particular program. For the first time ever, I began to consider the fact that there are innate programs.

The energy created within me, when the blocks were set together as a mandala, was one of the clues that led me to believe that it's in my intrinsic basic program to create from the center out. This is only one aspect of who I am, but it's a very important fact to know when I approach the design wall. Filling in the framework is not my way of working, nor is working from left to right or up to down. Understanding how to create collage designs is not the way my mind works, either. I create from the center out.

There is no right or wrong program, no right or wrong way to create. Your individual innate program is the important tool to use in developing your own personal style.

Miracle Windows, 1994. 48" x 48"

All the techniques and design tools that we have learned and will learn are filtered through our unique way of creating. Discover your own programming and then use this information to develop your own unique style.

I use my centered way of creating when I start a drawing, never knowing how it will evolve, but trusting in the program.

The key is to understand your innate program and to use it to develop a personal style, or as author Julia Cameron puts it, **"your vein of gold."**

Original sketch for *The Alchemist*

The Alchemist: Stirring the Elements, 2002. 80" x 80"

your creative style

Some people have an idea of what their personal style is, but have not thought of it as an innate program. Using this knowledge to nurture and enhance personal style will make a big difference in the creative process.

A place for quilters and artists to begin to gather information about their inborn natural program is to analyze the types or designs of quilts they have been attracted to over the years. Which quilts seem to send a burst of energy into your being when you first see them? If you keep a design idea folder, look through it. A pattern will probably evolve showing the designs you are attracted to; pay attention to this information. These may not necessarily be the style of quilts you have always made, but this strong attraction has a reason. It has to do with your innate creative style. You have a style, a talent and a purpose. You should use them. There is a purpose to the universe and if you do not use the talents you were given, you are cheating yourself and the world around you. There is no one else with the same unique vision as yours.

- An object from nature (i.e. rock, leaf, feather, shell, flower)
- 9" x 12" sketch pad (or larger)
- pencil
- see-through grid ruler, at least 12" long
- scissors

The following exercises are designed to give you some insight into your innate programming. There is no right or wrong answer, just your answer. Play. Stay open to where your energy or hand leads you.

Prepare and label six sheets of paper from a sketch pad as follows. Don't worry about exact measurements. Just get the lines on the paper.

Don't think! The slowest way to create is through the brain. Just feel and use your intuition.

general instructions

These instructions apply to all five exercises:

- Place object from nature on the table in front of you.
- Set aside all the sheets that do not pertain to the exercise that you are doing.
- Begin each creative session by closing your eyes, taking three deep breaths, quieting your brain and centering yourself. Allow your creative energy to begin to flow.
- Stay quiet for at least one minute or until you feel comfortable, then begin.
- You can cover the entire paper or any portion or section to which the drawing lines take you.
- Take about five minutes to do each drawing exercise.

1: leave blank

2: divide into 2" sections horizontally

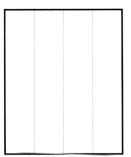

3: divide into 2" sections vertically

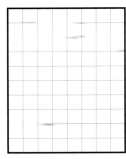

4: divide into 1" squares

5: divide into 2" × 3" squares

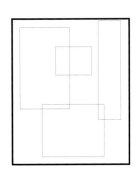

6. draw four rectangles and/or circles anywhere on the sheet. It is okay to overlap them; use more than one size. Place shapes where they feel comfortable to you.

Exercise 1

- Place the first blank sheet of paper in front of you in any position that feels comfortable.

- Open your eyes and study the nature object. Turn and examine it until you find lines that you would like to draw.

- Begin freehand drawing the lines or the entire object on the paper. Don't worry about being exact; improvise as you like.

Exercise 2

- Place the second sheet that contains the horizontal lines in front of you.

- Find a new angle or section on the nature object to draw.

- Begin drawing anywhere that feels comfortable on the paper.

Exercise 3

- Place the third sheet that contains the vertical lines in front of you.

- Find a different angle or section of the nature object to draw.

- Maybe this drawing wants to be contained in one vertical section or repeated in each section.

- Try to stay within the five-minute time frame.

Exercise 4

- Place sheets #4 (small squares) and #5 (large blocks) in front of you.
- It is important that you center yourself again before this exercise.
- Feel which sheet engages your energy.
- Use the sheet that attracted you the most and begin drawing your lines from the nature object.
- Fill in the square with a line or two in each square, or the entire sheet may be covered with one drawing.
- Just move through the squares in 5 minutes. Do not study and think—just feel.

Exercise 5

- Place sheet #6 (shapes) in front of you.
- Using lines from the nature object fill in the shapes on the paper. Each shape could contain different lines from the object. Enlarge, elongate, or reduce lines where desired.

Evaluating the drawings

- Hang all the drawings on your design wall.
- Take some time and view the drawings close-up and far away.
- This is not the time to worry about the actual composition of the design.
- Respond to the position of the drawing on the sheet and the lines on the sheet.

Questions to ask yourself

- Where did you start on each paper?
- Did you tend to start at the same place on all the drawings? Maybe you started in the center or possibly one of the corners.
- Did you tend to use all the space available or did you do little drawings?
- Did the lines help or hinder your ability to enjoy drawing?
- Was your drawing more detailed or representational?
- Was your energy engaged by the complexity of filling in many rectangles and/or circles on the sixth sheet?
- Which format felt the safest and most comfortable?
- Is the format comfortable because it is a learned style or does it also engage your energy?
- Is there one drawing that you cannot wait to go back to and develop into a composition?

Things to notice

- Some people use only a minute part of the surface available which would indicate that working in a smaller format works better for them.
- Always starting a drawing in a certain area (i.e. upper left hand) of the paper is useful information and can be the

starting point for all your drawing to evolve.

• Starting in the center could block your creative impulse or ignite your creative flame depending upon your innate style.

• Maybe starting at the bottom and designing up will give you the most powerful designs.

• Moving across the page creating images that flow may be your style.

• The small grid may have given you the opportunity to complicate the drawing and add more detail.

• The larger grid gives the opportunity to simplify and open up.

• Using the collage technique of pasting objects all over the surface can create movement and excitement for some artists.

• Information from a number of the different formats may unearth your style.

• One creative style may stand out only after you develop a full composition in each format.

Personal Examples

The best way I can explain how this evaluation works is to take you through the information I learned from these exercises.

• I always started in the center of the paper in each format.

• I felt uncomfortable with the vertical and horizontal formats.

Researching the subject of innate ways of thinking and creating is an exciting task.

• The small grid was more engaging because it gave me the opportunity to make an overall drawing more detailed.

• The large grid felt like it just wanted to have each square filled in and it left me cold.

• The numerous overlapping rectangles totally perplexed me. I wanted to view each rectangle individually and could not relate to them as a whole composition.

Summary

These exercises are a way to begin to understand your innate creative style. You may be lucky and immediately understand your attraction to one format. For others it will take repeating the exercises again and using a different object. Creating an inspiring environment with music can often deepen your creative state. Developing a full composition in each format may be what is needed to help one creative style stand out. Also, there are many variations of these formats to consider. I urge you to continue working with the ideas presented in this exercise as you design your future pieces. Keep in mind your personal style when trying any design format.

materials & supplies

- small format drawing
- large sheet of drawing paper (27" × 32" office flip charts, either plain or with a light background grid, work well)
- pencil & eraser
- Sharpie® ultra fine point marker
- large ruler

Developing the drawing

- Now is the time to look at your exercise drawings for composition.
- Just look at the drawings themselves. You can convert any drawing to your format.
- Choose the drawing that you like most.
- Enlarge the drawing freehand onto your prepared large sheet of paper.
- Develop the drawing into a full composition adding as many lines and elements as the design calls for.

Preparing the paper

- Use the format that you have identified as your preferred creative style to prepare a large sheet of paper (see supply list).
- If your large paper will require lines, grids or rectangles determine the size appropriate for the paper (i.e. a 4" grid of squares or lines 6" apart
- This is just an exercise so don't agonize about the size of the divisions.
- Use your ruler to lightly draw your lines on the paper.

Anything that can be drawn can be constructed in fabric.

Illustration 1: Hard lines are the original drawing. Dash lines indicate where the lines were extended to close shapes and make it easy to construct.

- Most drawings will have curved pieces. Options for constructing the curved piece compositions are: machine appliqué, fusing, piecing. (The following chapters contain construction methods for curved piece compositions.)

- Consider how constructible your composition is in fabric.

- You will most likely be creating templates of each piece. Lines ending in mid-air must be connected to another line to enclose the shape and make a template possible. *(Illustration 1)*

- For ease of construction consider dividing very large pieces into smaller sections. The sections can be created out of the same fabric to give the illusion of one large piece. *(Illustration 1)*

- Remember, fabric motifs can do some of the work of creating shapes ie: leaves or flowers.

- Some drawing lines can be enhanced with thread in the embellishment stage.

- When your drawing is complete, darken all lines with the Sharpie® marker. Number each piece and add registration marks throughout the drawing to help with accurate placement of each piece. *(Illustration 2)*.

General Examples

- A drawing may be done over the entire surface of a format, i.e., a vertical grid. The grid can then be developed with fabric, color and value changes across the surface.

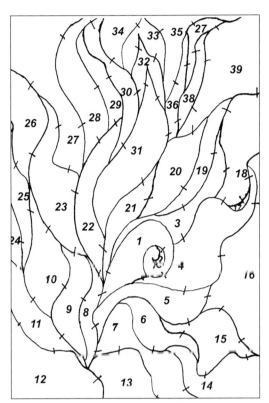

Illustration 2: Numbers and registration marks added. Registration marks show where to reconnect pieces

- Maybe replicating the same simple drawing in each section of the grid is needed.

- Piecing the straight lines and geometric shapes may fit some unique styles.

- Curved lines that flow and create movement may be what feeds your spirit.

- The collage format offers the opportunity to vary the size and shape of a drawing.

Individual concepts of how to develop a composition are infinite. Explore and manifest your unique vision.

Personal examples

- My designs always have a center or heart.

- If the drawing lines don't indicate a center, I create one with color choices and values.

- I lead the eye to the center with light. (i.e., horizontal format can still draw the viewer into the center.)

- Even my asymmetrical drawings have a center from where they evolved.

Original drawing for ***Vibrations of Spirit***

Vibrations of Spirit, 1998. 24" x 36"
Collection of Marjorie Taylor, Billings, MT

My innate style is creating powerful detailed images that evolve from a center or heart.

A Mother and Three Daughters: Compassion, 24" x 36", by Cynthia Taber, McCall, ID

Joy, by Linda Wolf Jackson, 39" x 32", Billings, MT
Style: **Left to right**

Alder, by Colleen Wise, 33" x 41", Puyallup, WA
Style: **Collage**

Emergence, by Nancy Porter, 37¾" x 32½",
Kirkland, WA
Style: **Center**

Dancing Orchid, by Carol Latham, 40" x 37",
Bainbridge Island, WA
Style: **Center**

Pretty Petals, by Karlyn Lohrenz,
54" x 56", Billings, MT
Style: **Collage**

Life is Sweet and Juicy, by Marsha Squires,
62" x 62", Fremont, CA
Style: **Vertical**

Selah Creek Bridge, by Cinda Langjahr,
85" x 44", Bellevue, WA
Style: **Horizontal**

Leaves of Another Year, by Darcy Faylor,
35" x 40", Bellevue, WA
Style: **Large grid**

the design unfolds

The design wall should be the focal point of any studio. It should be the first thing you see when you look into the room. That way, every time you walk into the studio, you get a new impression of the current piece evolving on the wall. Many times when a design is not talking to you or you are too close to the process, it helps to leave the room, take a few deep breaths, try to clear your mind and then reenter the room. Hopefully a new perspective will present itself. Sometimes it requires longer periods of time away from the design—days or even weeks—before the piece reveals what it needs next. The design wall is an integral tool in my design process. It allows me to audition fabrics and get some distance from the piece to see how the fabric reads. It helps me determine if a light fabric really reads as a medium or if a print might read as a solid. Space can help me see what the impact of the entire composition is at a distance. What looks like it works up close may not have the same visual impact once you step back.

- Pin the full size cartoon on the design wall.
- Choose an area to start on. (This will depend on your creative style, i.e., I always start in the middle).
- Pin template material on wall (if Sulky Totally Stable™; shiny side toward you) over the area that you have chosen.
- Do not trace all the templates for the entire piece before you start. This will allow you the option to edit later.

options for enlarging a small drawing

OPTION	PROS	CONS
Free hand drawing (which you have already done in previous chapter)	Easy, no machinery needed.	Taping paper together for large cartoon.
Enlarging a section at a time on a small copier.	Can be done on a home copier.	Tedious—enlarging a section at a time and then fitting and taping together to create full size cartoon.
Enlarging on a copier at a copy center that makes copies up to 36" wide and indefinite length.*	Attendant will usually help you or make copy for you. Can be enlarged in only a few sections for an image larger than 36" wide	More expensive.
Have a blueprint shop enlarge your drawing to your predetermined size or a percent enlargement.	Great for getting the exact size you want. They do the taping for you and you receive a very accurate cartoon.	More expensive (60" x 80" cartoon is about $75.00). They speak in mathematical/ percentage terms (sometimes they understand hand signals displaying approximate sizes).
Project the drawing to the size you want onto a large sheet of paper on the design wall and trace.	Can be done in the studio.	A projector must be purchased or rented.

*Copier and blueprint shops use percentages to enlarge. Ask the attendant exactly what size the enlarged drawing will be before making the copy. It helps to obtain the size you want and saves the expense of doing it twice.

- full-size cartoon
- template material; Sulky To-tally Stable™ is my choice.
- fabric: a variety of lights, mediums, and darks; batiks, prints, geometrics, hand-dyes, just to name a few.
- Sharpie® ultra fine point marker
- small sharp point scissors
- pins
- rotary cutter, ruler and mat
- optional: reducing glass

tip

Not everyone has a studio with a permanent design wall, but most of you can use a portable design wall hung in your sewing space. It may be a piece of white flannel or a flannel backed vinyl tablecloth. There are many materials that can be used to create a design wall. I have found that flannel or Pellon® Fleece (or a similar product) work the best because they allow pieces of fabric to stay in place without pins. Quilted portable design walls are also available and are great to take to workshops. (see Resources)

- •Completely trace the lines, registration marks and numbers that the template material covers with a Sharpie® marker.
- •Place traced template material on your table.
- •Cut out the first template piece of your choice right on the line.
- •Cut only the template you intend to work with. Too many precut pieces become easily misplaced.

The design wall is an integral tool in my design process.

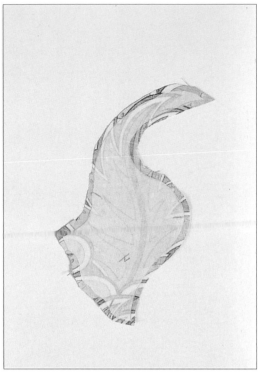

•With shiny, adhesive side down, lightly press the template onto the back of the chosen fabric.

•Cut around the template adding a ¼" all the way around.

•Leave template in place.

•Pin piece onto the cartoon over the corresponding number.

•If the fabric does not work as you had expected, just peel off the template and press it on your new fabric choice. The template can be reused many times.

•Continue the process for each template piece until the first section you chose to work on is designed.

Now it is on to the construction of

The process of doing only a section at a time allows for variations and redesigns as you go. Relax and play!

design elements, as opposed to looking at it as a whole piece.

• If the section of fabric that would work perfectly is in the middle of the fabric, don't hesitate to cut away.

• Commit to cutting and auditioning piece after piece until the right fabric is chosen.

• Use transition fabrics: pieces of fabric that contain colors that will help blend one piece into the next.

• Create your own fabric by machine-piecing strips of fabric into a panel from which templates will be cut.

• Your library of fabrics should contain a wide range of lights, mediums and darks; a variety of colors and textures; prints, solids, gradations, directional prints, transition and novelty fabrics; batiks, hand dyes, printed and painted fabrics.

the completed section (see next chapter). Once the section is sewn and positioned back on the wall you will be ready to continue with the design process.

Hints for choosing fabric

• Audition fabric on the wall to help make choices easier. Fold and pin the entire piece of fabric to be auditioned and pin on the wall in the section you are working on.

• Let your energy and intuition lead you and choose a fabric you love.

• Look at each piece of fabric for individual

I thought I would take you on the journey I took from working at my dining room table in 1986 to now, where I spend much of my time in a custom-designed 24' x 24' studio. Many of you can relate to one or more of my studio spaces along the way. Most did not come close to the definition of a studio, but I always had hopes there would be an actual studio someday.

In 1986, my "studio" consisted of an old Elna sewing machine on the dining room table. This was not a formal dining room, but it was our only eating space. My husband, Larry, and our three children, Scott, Darryl and Jennifer, often referred to the sewing machine at the end of the table as my fourth child. Fabric overflowed the table and was piled high on the chairs. My design wall was pinned to the drapes and the fabric was stored in plastic boxes under the bed. At that time, I did not need many boxes because I was still under the illusion that I should only buy fabric for a particular project—a limiting belief that I quickly overcame.

Then when my middle son left for the Army, his room became the sewing room. Although not an ideal space (it was downstairs and didn't have very good lighting), it was mine. An old kitchen

Photo by D. Tilton

table held my machine and the design wall was a more permanent fixture. The best feature of this room was a bookcase where I kept all my fabric boxes.

When my oldest son got married and moved out, I was free to take over the downstairs family room. This sewing room had more light, more space and room for more fabric.

Later we moved to a new, larger house. The 30'x 12' loft, in which three sides were entirely windows, became my space. While occupying this studio for four years, my work really took on new life and energy. I got a new Pfaff sewing machine and I was a happy camper. I was still working part-time as an interior designer and comptroller for my husband's corporation. My daughter was in junior high, so time spent on my art was still divided with many other tasks. I also devoted some of my time to teaching innovative quilting classes at my local quilt shop.

We moved again into another new house, one with a very unique environment filled with rich woods, slate rock and tile. The library was converted into my studio. It had lots of built-in bookcases for fabric and decent lighting, but was small.

Soon I started eyeing the large family room with a 32' wall of windows that filled the room with north light. A slate rock planter filled with greenery ran the length of the room, making it even more attractive. It offered a large space for a design wall, which

The space you work in does not have to limit your creativity.

provided a great perspective from at least 32 feet away. The problem was a very large, rarely used pool table that was kept in this room. The pool table was sold and all the family room furniture was rearranged into a small portion of the room, thus converting most of the family room into my new studio. I was able to create a wonderful studio, complete with new custom built sewing and cutting tables, a drafting table, and a new Pfaff 7570 (compliments of the Pfaff America professional consignment program). I also enjoyed this room because my family shared the space. I could work and we could talk; I no longer felt shut away from my family while working.

The space and working arrangement of this studio worked so well that when we purchased our hilltop home, the new studio space was designed to function just like the old space — with a small portion reserved as a family room. This, my current studio, is right off the kitchen, which is very convenient for me. Some artists dream of having solitary spaces, but I love being in the midst of my family and working at the same time.

My studio became a reality for me when I began to take my art seriously and focus on building a body of work. I quit my interior design and accounting positions. This was a large risk because my husband was the person I had to give my resignation to. I was not only leaving a job, but also quitting the dream that we would work together and build a successful business. As hard and upsetting as this was, it turned out to be an excellent change for both of us. He hired a CPA to replace me in the accounting position. Things began to run more smoothly for him and he got accurate reports on a regular basis. I am right-brained and never cared to adhere to a schedule. My attitude towards accounting was, "so what if the decimal point isn't in the right position?" I guarantee you would not want to hire me, a right-brained creative person, as your accountant.

When I was working as an accountant, I was doing somebody else's job. When I finally started doing my job, which was pursuing my art and using the gifts I was given, everybody benefited. I knew in the center of my being that if I did not honor and develop these talents, I would spend the rest of my life living the story imposed upon me by well-meaning family, teachers and friends. If I did not take action, I would never present the universe with the uniqueness I had to offer. Evidence that taking this risk was the right decision can be found in my passion to create and in my body of work.

Photo by D. Tilton

*what
now?*

Most freehand drawings contain curves, and yours will probably not be the exception. Not to worry! Anything that can be drawn can be constructed in fabric. Curves may require more than one method of construction. Threads and yarns are often another component used in developing the design. The challenge of bringing your design to life is an exciting process.

air appliqué

As the design unfolds and the energy begins to flow, the construction technique becomes secondary for me. As a visual person, I will do whatever I have to do to get the desired effect. Problem solving and finding a construction method that works for a particular design is just one more challenge that I enjoy. Problems are not obstacles, but opportunities to learn what works and what does not. I have made many attempts at constructions that were cumbersome and produced a mediocre product. Seasoned quilters and artists know many techniques so there is an abundance of knowledge to pull from. When what we know fails to do what we want, we need to search for a new method to accomplish the task. For those new to creating with fiber, the challenge may seem daunting. Sometimes there is an advantage in not knowing all the rules. It is easier to find innovative ways of constructing a piece when you have an open mind.

The method I most often use for curves is machine appliqué. In my experience it is a more forgiving and flexible method than machine piecing. Hand appliqué is an option for those who enjoy that process. Air Appliqué is the method that will be described in this chapter. Air appliqué means appliquéing one piece to another without the aid of a foundation.

In the process of constructing fiber pieces with machine appliqué, I have found products and techniques that allow me to sew with greater precision. Although art pieces are about a visual image, the technique needs to support and enhance the image. Construction techniques that are poorly executed detract from the beauty of the quilt. The methods and tools used in this exercise are the ones I use in my own art quilts.

Oxymoron: Planned Serendipity, 2001. 30" x 48"

Air appliqué means appliquéing one piece to another without the aid of a foundation.

materials & supplies

- sewing machine
- open toe embroidery foot
- needles: embroidery 80/12, Microtex 90/14, Jeans Stitch 70/10
- thread: invisible or nylon lingerie/bobbin
- repositionable glue stick (Clover® or Scotch® Brand)
- embroidery scissors

tip

The smallest width setting on my machine is 2.0, which is too wide. To obtain the correct width I set my width at 3.0 and engage the double needle function which reduces the width in half to 1.5.

The Sewing Machine

- Should be clean and in good operating order.
- You should be familiar with your machine and its capabilities.
- At minimum, the machine must have a zigzag stitch with adjustable length and width.
- Newer machines have pre-programmed utility and decorative stitches.
- A blanket or blind hemstitch works well for invisible machine appliqué.
- Decorative stitches can be used with colored thread for an added design element.

Sewing Machine Set Up

Setting up the sewing machine is one of the most important factors in achieving a great invisible appliqué stitch. Each machine brand and model offers different settings. Experiment with your machine by sewing test strips until you find the right combination of stitch, tension, setting, needle, top thread and bobbin thread.

Invisible Appliqué Stitch:
The width should be wide enough, about 1/8 inch, to just catch the fabric when it "bites" over, and the length should be short enough to secure it nicely.

Presser Foot:
Most machines recommend a presser foot for each particular stitch. An open-toed foot is my choice.

invisible appliqué stitch:

STITCH	QUALITY	ILLUSTRATION	WIDTH	LENGTH
blanket stitch	best	⊔⊔⊔⊔⊔⊔⊔⊔	1.5	1.5
	too small	⊔⊔⊔⊔⊔⊔⊔⊔⊔⊔⊔⊔	.5	.5
	too large	⊔ ⊔ ⊔ ⊔ ⊔ ⊔	3.0	3.0
blind hem		_ _/_ _/_ _/_		
zig zag		/\/\/\/\/\/\/\/\		
decorative		/_/_/_/_/_/_/_ XXXXXXXX		

 tip Once you achieve a good stitch, record the machine settings, needle, and thread information for future reference.

Needles:
The needle size and type will usually depend on the type of fabric and thread you are using. Be willing to change the needle to the best size or type often if your composition contains a number of different types of fabrics. Hand-dyed fabrics sometimes require a Jeans Stitch needle to puncture the surface effectively and obtain a smooth stitch.

Threads:

Good quality invisible thread should be used. Lingerie/bobbin thread or 60 wt. fine thread in the bobbin produces a smooth, less bulky stitch. This thread is a lighter weight than regular sewing thread. The top tension needs to be loosened, while the bobbin tension usually needs to be tightened.

Each sewing machine is different and will respond differently to threads and fabrics. Run test strips and when you find the right combination, record the results.

threads

FABRIC	NEEDLE	TOP THREAD	BOBBIN THREAD
Commercial 100% Cotton	Embroidery 00/12	YLI® or Sulky® invisible thread	YLI® lingerie/bobbin thread Superior-The Bottom Line™
Batiks (a tighter weave)	Microtex 90/14	YLI® or Sulky® invisible thread	YLI® lingerie/bobbin thread Superior-The Bottom Line™
Hand Dyed	Jeans Stitch 70/10	YLI® or Sulky® invisible thread	YLI® lingerie/bobbin thread Superior-The Bottom Line™

To check for correct bobbin tension:

- Hold the thread end and let the bobbin dangle.
- Give it a light, quick jerk.
- The jerk should cause bobbin to fall a short distance easily and stop.
- Tension is too tight if the bobbin does not fall easily.
- Tension is too loose if the bobbin falls a long distance or does not stop falling.

Scissors:

Scissors will be needed for cutting out the Sulky Totally Stable™ templates and clipping curves. No matter what type of scissors you use, very sharp points are a must when clipping curves. Fiskars Softouch® scissors have an easy grip handle. I prefer their micro-tip or embroidery scissors.

Constructing the Curves

- Begin by taking the first two pieces off the wall.
- Note where the edges of the two pieces connect.

- Determine which piece you want on top.
- One will overlap the other and the seam allowance on the bottom piece will *not* be turned under where they connect/overlap.
- The seam allowance of the top piece will be folded over on the connecting edge of the template.
- Clip the curves of the edge to be folded over the template
- Lay the top piece face down, and using a repositionable glue stick, glide a thin line of glue on the fabric at the edge you want to fold over the template.
- Fold edge over the template.

> **tip**
>
> Repositionable glue stick is water soluble and has a temporary bond. It allows the seam to be repositioned and the template to be reused if necessary.

- Put a little glue on the underside of the folded edge and position on top of the lower piece matching registration mark.
- Pieces should fit together snugly, like a puzzle.

•Sew slowly with appliqué stitch.

•Be sure the straight stitching line lays close to, but not on top, of the folded edge. Only a few threads should be caught in the "over-bite" part of the stitch.

•Continue adding pieces until the entire section is completed.

•Pin back in place on the wall.

•Do not remove the Sulky Totally Stable™ templates until an entire piece is constructed and ready to layer with backing and batting.

•With curved pieces you are dealing with many bias edges, so leaving the templates in place until the design is complete will reduce the chance of stretching and distortion.

Adding air appliqué to your tool chest of techniques opens the door to designing quilts with feeling and spontaneity.

A complicated design is no problem with this tool to draw upon. Have fun and enjoy the process.

voices from the wall

Do your quilts talk to you? My quilts talk to me! In fact, they are quite obstinate in demanding my attention. Quilts talk if you are listening. When you listen—when you are responsive to the design as it develops on the wall—glorious images begin to emerge. As you begin a drawing you usually have an idea in mind. The drawing starts along the line of the original idea with a quiet conversation going on between the pencil and the paper. Then, the conversation begins in earnest when you start composing with the fabric and color on the wall. As the new energy of color and light enters the picture the design takes on a voice of its own.

evolution of a design

This is the point where we need to step back and observe the image. Does it want to continue as planned; or is there something new emerging that could not have been foreseen in the original design? Have the lines become more graphic or are they subtle and playful? Are the colors changing to deeper and richer hues or changing to different colors completely? Often the image requires a change in shape and size. My pieces usually grow larger to do the image justice.

If you listen and get your everyday brain out of the way, all the information you need to create a unique, powerful image is available right on the wall in front of you. This process is not about an educated eye for design, it is about intuition! Each and every one of us is intuitive. As I have said before, the slowest way to create is by thinking; the fastest way is by feeling and intuition. Stop often as the design evolves and feel the direction it wants to go. When I try to impose my original design idea on an evolving quilt, the end product is usually only a shell of what it could have been. If the process becomes combative and unsatisfyng it is a clue that I am not listening. I need to get out of the way and let the quilt develop however it wants. Joy and peace then return to the design process.

Make your first priority to create with joy and freedom. Trust your own creative feelings and respond to the piece at each stage of the process. Interpreting the design according to technical and academic rules is secondary. Only when the energy of the design is in place, do you begin to look to design principles for help in developing the image into a balanced composition.

We will take the process step-by-step and see how a design evolves. *A Bird Of Another Color* will be used to illustrate this process. This piece speaks not only to the design, but to the innate fabric of my being. I am an alchemist at heart—I love the process of taking one thing and changing it to another. Transforming an idea, renovating a home, or designing environments are all alchemical processes. Taking an idea, fabric and thread and transforming them into an art quilt is like turning iron into gold. All artists and quilters must have a little alchemist in them. Let us proceed and transform an idea together.

Emergence, 2003. 24" x 24"

Photo by D. Tilton

Evolution of a design

Consider recording the evolution of your design with a camera. A digital camera and computer make it easy to view images right away. A photographic series of the design process gives you information about how the design looks from a distance. Are the fabric and color choices giving you the contrast and energy you desire? There comes a time, usually early in the process, when you view the evolving design and you know if it wants to "*stay on the original path or change direction.*" If you are unsure at this point continue on the original path. The design can be changed at any time along the path.

Staying on the original path

- Begin another section.
- Place Sulky Totally Stable™ to cover the new section and slightly overlap the completed section.

 tip   Sulky Totally Stable™ is transparent enough to see the fabric image and underlying cartoon.

- The overlap is necessary due to possible distortion caused by pieces not accurately sewn together in the first section.
- Trace 1/4" inside the edge of the completed fabric image.
- Complete tracing all the lines of the new chosen section.

- Continue the design process until this section is complete.
- Once you are happy with a section, machine appliqué pieces together leaving templates in place.
- Sew it to the first section.
- Continue constructing sections until the design is complete.
- Add borders or other elements, as desired, to complete the top.
- *Do not* remove the template material until the entire design is complete including borders.
- When removing the templates do not try to get every little piece out of the points. It is better to have a little paper under the seam than to break the stitched seam while removing it.
- A warm iron helps release the templates.
- Press and square up the completed top.
- Blocking can be done if the piece is distorted.

Changing direction

Is the piece talking to you? What direction does it want to go? You may need to leave the room and clear your energy. When you return you should have a fresh perspective on what is happening on the wall. Use your camera as necessary.

So your design has spoken and wants to change direction. The original cartoon will no longer be your guide. If you are uncertain of the new direction or if new lines are needed, go back to the drawing board.

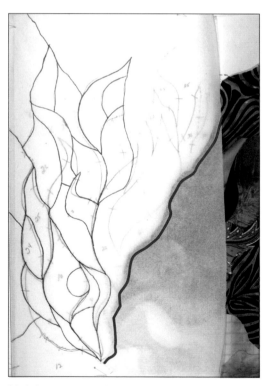

Black lines are original drawing. Red lines are redraft.

Options for changing the design

- If you used a digital camera download the current image of the design. Print three or four copies of the image on your computer printer. Sketch ideas on the copies.

- Sketch ideas on paper if digital images are not available.

- Lay tracing paper over the original drawing and play with possible changes.

- When you are ready to make changes on the wall, pin a large piece of Sulky Totally Stable™ over the area to be redesigned.

- Outline 1/4" inside the adjoining edge of the completed fabric section. See red line.

- Freehand the design changes on the template paper.

- Continue designing and listening. You will often feel energized at this point by the conversation between you and your quilt.

- Do only one section at a time because the design may continue to change.

 tip
Do not over-think changes to the design. Feel what is there and add to it.

This design wanted to be birds, not flowers.

- Photograph the piece at each stage of the design to get a better perspective of how the design is evolving.

Adding the background elements

- Do you have a central image requiring the support of a background? Some images are an all-over design and a definite background is unnecessary.

- It could be time to either go back to the drawing board or just audition background fabric choices.

- The background should support the image and become an integrated part of the whole piece.

For example, the original drawing might call for a geometric background, but when you try to impose the geometric background on the design it becomes the predominate element. It may be too strong for the image. Beautiful multi-colored hand dyed fabric might be just what is needed to enhance the central image. The two separate design elements—the image and the background—should become one integrated image.

Back Lighting:
Create a glow emanating from behind the image.

Deep Space:
Dark shading, pulling you into the image.

Implied:
A continuation of the image in more subtle tones.

Active:
Design elements that create movement and lead the viewer throughout the piece.

Juxtapose:
Geometric shapes that contrast the curves of a central image.

Graduations:
Lead and play with subtle color changes.

options: background effects

Completing the design

The addition of borders can make or break a design. All the considerations that you have given your design up to this point are still needed when choosing the finishing elements. The conversation is not yet over. Listen and audition!

- Proportion is important when choosing a border.

- Borders are a continuation of the design.

- Repeating some of the shapes, elements, and colors helps create an integrated composition.

- Have you listened to your quilt? Does it need or want a border?

- If you are still unsure, set the piece aside, and do the exercise in the "Begin at the End" chapter.

Remember, this is just the quilt top; the textural elements are yet to come. Each step along the way breathes more life into the piece. Continue to document the evolution in pictures. Where there was nothing, there is now an amazing piece of art created by you.

A Bird of Another Color wanted an extension of the central image. It needed a contrasting strip to separate the extension from the center. This gave it an implied border.

There is one hazard I must tell you about when informing non-quilt artists that your quilts talk to you; they may take you literally.

While being interviewed by a local newspaper about my design process, I said that I listen to my quilts. Elaborating, I added that my quilts talk to me and direct the evolution of the design.

When the article appeared my daughter—who was a junior in high school at the time—was pulled aside by her English teacher. The teacher asked if everything was okay at home. She expressed concern for my daughter's well-being in a home environment where quilts talk to her mom. My daughter explained the creative process and described how magnificent pieces of art have been created by listening to the work. The teacher dismissed the explanation and offered the assistance of the counselors if Jennifer ever needed help.

Not everyone understands the creative process. I hope you now have experienced the reward of listening to your designs. The conversation between artist and the image is a gift.

A Bird of Another Color, 2004. 32" x 45"

the challenge of spirals

I enjoy the problem-solving aspect of developing a composition. When I am perplexed and feel as if I have designed myself into a corner, I let my intuition take over and glorious solutions present themselves. These design solutions often require innovative construction methods. This was the case during the creation of *In The Beginning*.

The question: "How do I draw and construct this spiral?"

In the Beginning began with the black and white sharp-pointed outer ring. Next came the idea for a black and white spiral of points for the center. The question was "How do I draw and construct this spiral?" Who should know better than an engineer? I had two to call upon; friend and fellow quilter John Flynn and my husband, Larry. John gave me advice in mathematical terms. I nodded my head a lot and pretended to understand him and left completely confused. My next stop was my husband's office. More of the same mathematical language and formulas. In a pleading voice I asked, "Will you please help me do the actual drawing?" An entire day of drawing with my husband gave me a perfect spiral and points. I should say, an entire *torturous* day of drafting. My brain just does not work that way and I could not create another spiral using that method if my life depended on it.

Spirals are a universal symbol.

I love spirals. They create such powerful designs. There had to be an easier way to draft spirals. My search began. Freehand drawing was an option I used when creating *Genesis Revisited*. It was okay, but it wasn't very accurate. I finally discovered circular graph paper at an architectural/engineering supply store. There is also a web site where you can download a graph paper printing program. Designing became so much easier and faster. The following pages detail the process of creating spirals using circular graph paper.

Detail from **Genesis Revisited**

In The Beginning, 1994. 60" X 60"
Collection of Karey Bresenhan

drafting spirals

Begin with circular grid or graph paper. Use a fine lead mechanical pencil. A colored lead will help the dots stand out.

materials & supplies

- circular grid or graph paper available in architect/engineering supply stores. A shareware graph paper printing program (Windows only) is available at http://perso.easynet.fr/~philimar/graphpapeng.htm
- fine-lead mechanical pencils; regular and colored lead
- eraser
- Sharpie® ultra fine point marker
- ruler: see-through and at least 12" long

terms: spirals

Radiating Line:
a straight line that extends from the center to the outer edge of the paper

Radiating Section:
the area between two radiating lines

Circles:
begin in the center and get progressively bigger as they move out toward the outer edge

Circular Section:
the area between two circles

Points:
are drawn in the area between the inner and outer drawn spiral and look like a saw tooth

Solutions often require innovative designs and construction methods.

Drafting the outer spiral

- Freehand draw the beginning of the spiral from the center to the first circle (lines are too small to count). Place a dot.

- Now you will use sections and circles to develop a spiral.

- Continue the spiral beginning with the first dot.

- Count over two sections from the first dot and diagonally up to the second circle, place a dot in upper right corner.

- Continue this marking sequence over two sections and up one circle and placing a dot in the upper right corner until you reach the outer edge.

- Connect the dots freehand moving progessively outward to draft a spiral.

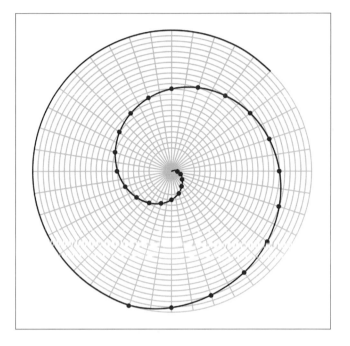

Drafting the inner spiral

- From the point that the outer spiral intersects the first circle count back counterclockwise five sections and place a dot.

- Again freehand the beginning of the spiral from the center to the dot on the first circle.

- Count over three sections and diagonally up one circle; place a dot in the upper right corner.

- Continue the sequence over three sections and up one circle and place a dot in the upper right hand corner until you meet the outer spiral.

- Connect the dots freehand, moving progessively outward to draft a spiral.

- Use a marking pen to darken the spiral lines.

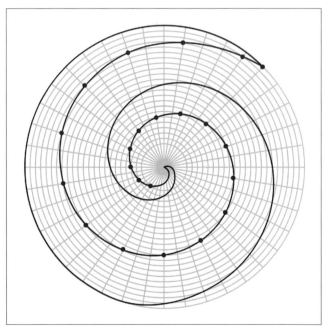

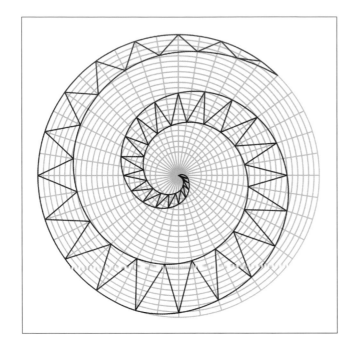

Adding the points

- Leave the center section where you free-hand drew the spiral until last.

- Use the dots on the inner circle for the base of the points.

- All the points are two sections wide at the base.

- Using a ruler and your marker, draw a line from the first dot on the inner spiral up to the center section line where it intersects with the outer spiral.

- Draw a line from the second dot to meet the last line you drew at the outer spiral forming a point two sections wide at the base.

- Continue drawing in all the points.

- Go back to the center and freehand draw in a few points.

- You now have one complete spiral with points. This is called the geometric spiral.

Different sequences create a variety of sizes and shaped spirals. The graph paper makes it easy to play and experiment with spirals.

Drafting the radiating spiral

As you look at your drawing you see a spiral and outer edges of the paper that have no lines drawn in yet. The lines outside the spiral will now be added to complete the drawing.

• Never draw the radiating line through the geometric spiral, always skip over it.

• Place your ruler on the center dot and on any corner of the paper.

• Draw the line, using your marker, from the center to the geometric spiral, stop, skip over the spiral and continue drawing line on the other side of the spiral until it meets the geometric spiral again, stop, skip the spiral again and continue the line out to the corner.

• Count over two sections and draw the next radiating line from the center to the edge.

• Continue until all the radiating lines are drawn. You now have a complete pattern.

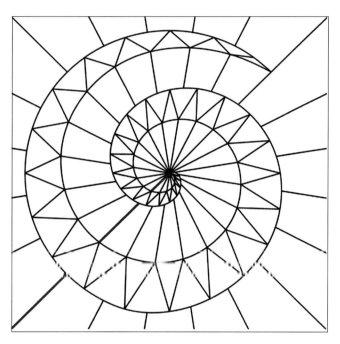

This drawing can be enlarged 600% to make an 18" block

options

• Different sequences create a variety of sizes and shapes of spirals, i.e., over one/up one would create a very tight spiral while over four/up two would make your spiral very wide.

• The inner and the outer spiral sequences can be varied.

• More than one spiral can be drawn from the center on a page.

• Points can be any size, i.e., narrow, tall points or fat, short points.

• The graph paper makes it easy to play and experiment with spirals.

• Eliminate the radiating lines and impose the geometric spiral on a background fabric.

• Spirals are a universal symbol and many published images can be used for inspiration. Do not copy images that are copyrighted.

The method I use when constructing spirals is foundation piecing and it works very well. This section walks you through my method for foundation piecing geometric and radiating spirals.

materials & supplies

FOR AN 18" BLOCK:

- foundation 1 yard Sulky Totally Stable™ at least 18" wide.
- Sharpie® ultra fine point marker
- rotary cutter and mat
- see-through grid ruler, at least 12" long
- basic sewing supplies
- sewing machine
- 80/12 embroidery needle
- black thread
- repositionable glue stick

Fabric:

- 1/4 yard each of black & white fabric
- 20 1/8 yard pieces of five colors. Each color should have lights, mediums and darks. Batiks, multi-colored fabrics and small prints work well. For more variety and choices add more fabrics in each color range.

- Enlarge drawing 600% on copier to an 18" block.

Cutting the fabric strips

- Cut one strip of black and one strip of white in each of the following sizes:
  - 1" x 42"
  - 2" x 42"
  - 3" x 42"

If you need more or larger strips cut them as needed.

Sewing machine setup

- Black thread on top and in the bobbin
- 80/12 needle
- Shorten the stitch length to 2.0. This helps perforate the foundation for easy removal.

Making the template

- Tape your enlarged spiral drawing to the table.

- Tape a piece of Sulky Totally Stable™ shiny side up (or a lightweight stitch and tear stabilizer) on top of the pattern.

- Trace all the dark spirals, points and radiating lines and the outside edges of the block.

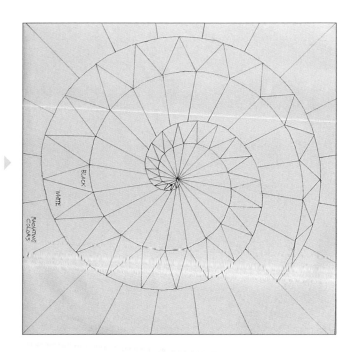

 The adhesive quality of Sulky Totally Stable™ is not needed in this process, but I like its transparent quality and soft but strong flexibility.

Cut out geometric spiral. Insert point of scissors into the end of the spiral and cut out on inside line of spiral and on outside line of spiral. *Do not cut through the outside edge to get to the radiating spiral.*

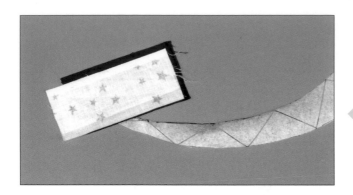

Piecing the geometric spiral

- Lay the geometric spiral on the table in front of you traced side up.

- Start with the tail end of the spiral.

- Strips are always placed on the traced side and sewing is done on the reverse side.

- Lay a 3" wide black fabric strip face up on top of the 1st section.

- Fabric should completely cover the section with at least 1/2" extension on either side of the spiral.

- Position a 3" white fabric strip face down on top of the black fabric.

- Make sure that you have allowed enough white fabric to cover the next section. To check this, fold the white fabric open as it would be after stitching and it should cover the next section.

- Hold or pin fabric in place, flip to the reverse side and stitch right on the first line.

- Trim stitched seam allowance to 1/8".

- Flip right side up and finger press open.

  Important: Do not iron—finger press only. Sulky Totally Stable™ is fuseable. Also, the iron will distort the spiral.

- Cut off the excess fabric strip for easy positioning of next fabric by:

    1. Flipping to reverse side.

    2. Fold back the template right on the next stitching line.

    3. Position ruler with the 1/4" line right on top of the folded edge.

    4. Use rotary cutter to trim along ruler edge.

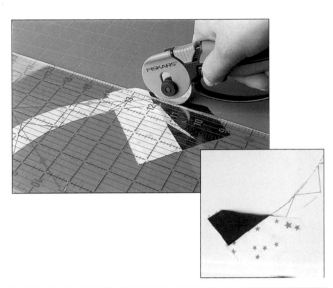

- Flip right side up and position 3" black strip face down on top of white strip.

- Stitch this section from the reverse side as before.

- Continue this process of placing, flipping, sewing and trimming to complete the spiral design. *Make sure you do not skip a line, always sewing on the next line of the spiral. Note: It's a matter of choice whether you have a black base of points on the inner edge and white base on the outer edge or white on the inner and black on the outer edge.*

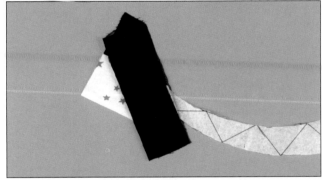

- At some point in the process, 3" strips are no longer necessary. Switch to 2" strips and then to 1" strips as it becomes evident that the strips are too large.

- After the spiral is completed, lay the entire template face down. Trim outside edges of fabric leaving at least 1/2" seam allowance past the edge of the template on each side.

Piecing the radiating spiral

The radiating spiral is done with the same foundation-piecing technique: place, flip, sew, trim, and finger press.

options: radiating spirals

Smooth Gradations:
Gradually transition from one color to the next, being careful to not make an abrupt transition.

Pinwheel:
Abrupt change that stops the flow between each color

Undulation:
Create a sequence. Vary strip widths and shading, i.e., light-medium-dark-medium-light.

- Audition color placement and gradations on the wall by placing black & white spirals on the wall and then pinning up possible color choices around it.

- Start with center fabric color and add gradations of that color.

- Use as many different pieces of each color as you want.

- It is easier to combine two or three of the tiny section at the beginning of the spiral into one.

- Five color gradations in the center of the spiral might equal about 1". Five color gradations at the end of the spiral might equal 4".

- Consider doing more of the center colors to balance out the transitions.

- Sometimes one multi-colored fabric will work for two or three sections.

- When you are ready to add the next color, find a transition color fabric (a fabric containing the color of a section you are transitioning from and the color you are transitioning to).

- Adding next fabric at the end of the tail: position a piece of fabric large enough to cover the long next section.

- Flip to reverse side and stitch only on line that is covered by both fabrics.

- The top section of the line is left unsewn so you have a floppy piece of fabric for a while.

- Continue adding fabrics until the end of the spiral.

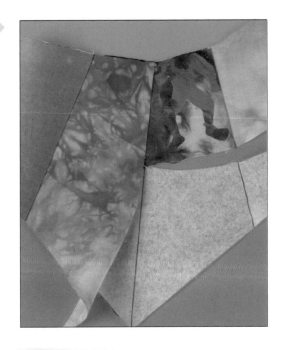

- The edge of the last fabric you add at the end of the spiral is placed under the loose fabric piece.
- The edge of the top fabric is folded under and machine appliquéd over the bottom piece.
- When complete, lay template face down and trim edges leaving at least 1/2" past the edge of the template on each side.

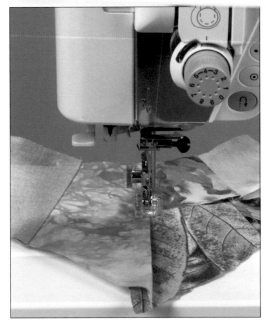

Combining the geometric and radiating spirals

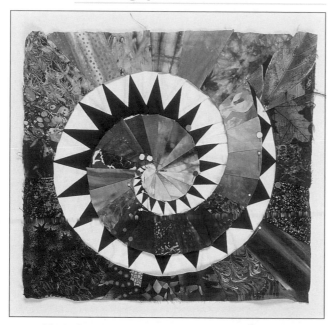

- The radiating spiral will be machine appliquéd on top of the geometric spiral.

- Lay the radiating spiral face down and glue and fold all the spiral edges.

- Position the two spirals together.

- Place a pin through exact center of the top spiral and then into the center of the bottom spiral and secure. Do the same on the tail end.

- The center of the radiating spiral, with all its bulk, sometimes needs to be coaxed into place with a lot of glue and a stilleto.

- Start pinning in place from the center, stop after securing about three inches.

- Next pin about three inches of the tail section.

- Stop and go back to the middle and continue pinning another few inches.

- Continue this back and forth pinning process until the entire spiral is flat and pinned together.

- Machine appliqué pinned block together, and remove paper.

- Trim block to 16 1/2".

tip

Do not try to start pinning the spiral at one end and go all the way to the end; it rarely fits. By working from both ends to the center, it allows the pieces to be eased together.

Genesis Revisited, 1997. 68" × 78"

organic spirals

Now the fun begins. Experience the winding, twisting lines as they flow into a free-form spiral shape. Let your hand and pencil lead you wherever they want to go. No more rulers, no more sharp points—draw free-flowing lines. If you love the spiral form, this is a simpler way to design and construct this powerful image. Intricate, bold, graphic spirals can be included in your compositions without drafting.

Drawing an organic spiral

Flexibility is the key element when designing this spiral.

It can be any shape, any size, or any dimension that you would like. Let yourself play! Do many drawings to experience a variety of spiral shapes. You have flexibility when designing the shape of the spiral, and the divisions can also be any size or shape. They can be skinny or fat, numerous or few, balanced or irregular.

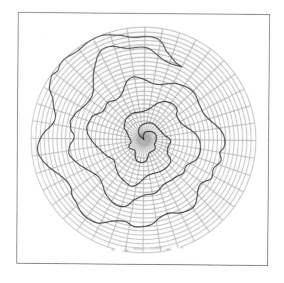

• Freehand draw organic spirals on circular graph paper using a mechanical pencil.

• Add divisions instead of points.

materials and supplies

• circular grid graph paper
  8 1/2" ×11" / available
  in architect/engineering
  supply stores or a graph
  paper printing program is
  available at:
  http://perso.easynet.
  fr/~philimar/graphpapeng.
  htm

• fine lead mechanical pencil

• eraser

• Sharpie® ultra fine point
  marker

• ruler
  see-through, at least 12"
  long

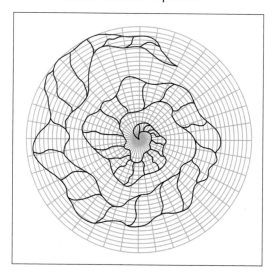

- Freeform, organic, radiating lines may be needed in your design., instead of straight lines.

Drawing the radiating lines

- Do not draw the radiating line through the spiral; always skip over it.

- Place the ruler on the center dot and on an outside corner of the paper.

- Draw the line with your marker from the center to the spiral edge, stop, and skip over the spiral. Continue drawing the line from the other side of the spiral to the next edge of the spiral; stop, skip over the spiral and continue to the outside edge.

- You have flexibility in this phase of the design. See options above.

- Continue until all the radiating lines are drawn.

- Number the sections inside the spiral.

- Darken all lines with the marker.

- Enlarge design on copier to desired size. An 18" block is used for this exercise.

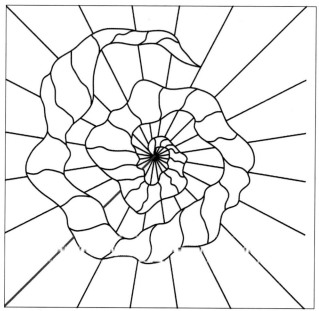

Can be enlarged 600% to an 18" block.

Radiating Line:
the line that extends from the center to the outer edge of the paper

Radiating Section:
the area between two radiating lines

Circles:
begin in the center and get progressively bigger as they move out.

Circular Section:
the area between two circles

Divisions:
the wavy lines drawn in the area between the inner and outer spirals

FOR AN 18" BLOCK:

- template material:
  1 yard Sulky Totally Stable™
  at least 18"

- Sharpie® ultra fine point
  marker

- rotary cutter and mat

- ruler: see-through and at
  least 12" long

- basic sewing supplies

- sewing machine

- 80/12 embroidery needle

- black thread

- repositionable glue stick

- fabric:
  1/4 yard black
  1/4 yard white
  20 (1/8 yard) pieces of five
  colors. Each color should
  have lights, mediums and
  darks. Batiks, multi-colored
  fabrics and small prints
  work well. For more variety
  add more fabrics in each
  color range. The leftover
  colored fabric from the
  previous chapter can be
  used for this project.

Preparation for machine appliqué

- Tape the enlarged spiral drawing to the
  table in front of you.

- Position a sheet of Sulky Totally Stable™, a
  little larger than the spiral itself and shiny
  side up, on the drawing.

First template

- Using a marker, trace the spiral lines and
  the divisions. Do not trace the numbers
  within the spiral or the radiating lines.

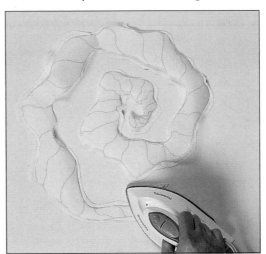

- Cut out the spiral.

- Press the template, shiny/adhesive side
  down, on reverse side of white fabric.

- Cut out, adding 1/4" seam allowance all
  the way around.

- When this spiral is face up the template section lines will be slightly visible
  through the fabric. They will be used as
  guides for positioning the black pieces.

When using the shiny side of the Sulky Totally Stable™, you do not have to work in mirror image.

Second Template

- Lay a second piece of Sulky Totally Stable™, the size of the entire drawing, shiny side up, on the drawing.

- Trace all the lines, divisions, numbers and radiating lines, including the spiral and the outside edge of the block again.

- Cut out the organic spiral. Do not cut in from the edge of the paper (p. 79, bottom photo).

- Set radiating spiral aside.

- Cut out sections 1, 2, 3, 4 & 5 from the spiral. Do just a few at a time; they get lost.

- Set the even-numbered sections aside.

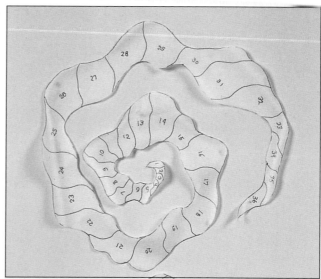

The even-numbered pieces can be used as a reference guide for placing the black odd-numbered section on the white spiral if necessary..

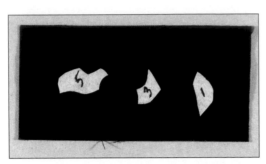

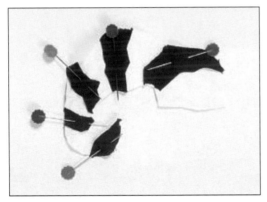

• Place section #1, #3, and #5 shiny/adhesive side down on the back of the black fabric and press.

• Cut out #1 section with a 1/4" seam allowance all the way around.

• Glue and turn the edge of adjoining #2 piece (not the tail sides).

• Position section #1, according to the pattern, on the solid white spiral.

• Glue or pin in place.

• These division lines are slightly visible on the white spiral. Use these for proper placement.

• If the division lines are not visible use the even-numbered pieces for correct placement of black divisions.

• Cut out section #3. Glue and turn the edges adjoining #2 and #4.

• Position section # 3; glue in place.

• Machine appliqué sections in place.

• Continue using the same process of adding odd-numbered black pieces to the spiral.

• Set the completed spiral aside.

tip

If the section lines are not visible through the white spiral prepare for adding section #3, lay paper section #2 in position, aligning edges with section #1.

Radiating spiral

Create and foundation piece the radiating spiral using directions in previous chapter.

Combining the organic and radiating spirals

- The radiating spiral will be machine appliquéd on top of the organic spiral.

- Lay radiating spiral face down and glue and fold the spiral edges under.

- Position the two spirals together (see p. 84).

- Place a pin through exact center of the top spiral and then into the center of the bottom spiral and secure. Do the same on the tail end.

- Start pinning in place from the center, stop after securing about three inches.

- The radiating spiral, with all its bulk, sometimes needs to be coaxed into place with glue and a stiletto.

- Next, pin about three inches of the tail section, stop and go back to the other end and do another few inches.

- Continue this back and forth pinning process until the entire spiral is flat and pinned together.

- Machine appliqué both sections together and remove paper.

- Trim block to 16 1/2".

options

- Make a one-block wall hanging.
- Make a mandala quilt using a block as the center.
- Make a whole quilt of the same or alternating blocks.
- Blocks can be sashed or floated.
- Set the blocks on point.
- Make a Cosmic Spirals (see photo and instructions on next page).

Cosmic Spirals, 1999. 62" x 34"

Combining the geometric & organic blocks

materials

Fabric:
1/2 yard cosmic fabric: a cosmic or mottled fabric containing most of the colors used in the radiating section works well and gives the illusion of floating blocks.

- Add a 2" black strip to top and bottom of geometric spiral block.

- Add a 2" white strip to each side of the geometric spiral block.

- Miter corners.

- Repeat on the organic spiral reversing the position of the black and white strips.

- Piece the two blocks together.

- Add a 3" or 4" floating strip of cosmic (multi-colored) fabric around the blocks.

- Add the border of your choice or try a checkerboard or an optical checkerboard border (see Resources).

Now that you have the technique down for the organic spiral, it is time to get creative. Let your imagination lead you. Design a quilt full of the organic shapes or worms as I call them. Let the spirals take you into deep space as in the piece *Time Warp*. The totality of possibilities is available when you engage your creative spirit. Karlyn, Ionne and Carol let their imaginations blossom into these beautiful quilts.

Choices, 21" x 21"
by Carol Seeley, Campbell River, BC, Canada

Wild Thing, 24" x 24"
by Karlyn Bue Lohrenz, Billings, MT

Cruise Control, 24" x 24"
by Ionne McCauley, Qualicum Beach, BC, Canada

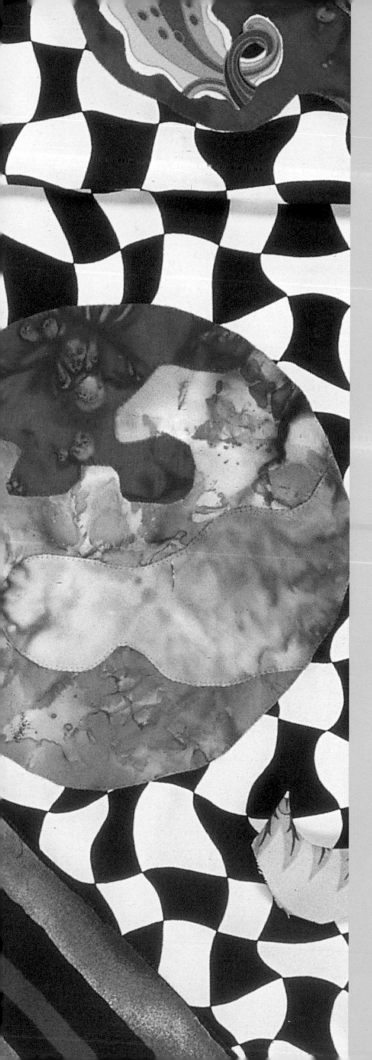

begin at the end

Are you ready to begin your next quilt by designing the border first? The goal is to achieve a totally integrated design by opening up a conversation between the main body of the quilt and the border. Try it and give yourself an entirely new perspective on the design process. This is definitely a right brain experience with new possibilities presenting themselves in unexpected ways while you design this small art quilt.

If you are like me, many times the border is just an afterthought. When the top is completed, the energy of my design process is winding down. The border often does not get the attention it deserves. Other times the top does not have the quality of energy I would like, so I try to add unique elements in the border that will bring the total piece to life. This can result in a disjointed image. These unique border elements are frequently more innovative than my central design and often find themselves in my next quilt. This exercise has helped my body of work evolve. Your unsuccessful designs can be just as important as your masterpieces when developing your creative voice.

My design process is built on an evolving design rather than following a complete drawing to the end. So how was I to achieve a beautifully integrated image? What if? What if I start with a border drawing and then bring some of the elements and shapes into the main body of the quilt? It was worth a try. So began a new adventure that has enhanced the quality of my work. The process is not one I use all the time; but when my designs are lackluster, I revert to this process to push my thinking out of the box again.

materials and supplies

- large sheet of drawing paper 26" x 32"(Office Flip Chart, 27" x 33" with graph lines, trimmed to above size works well).
- 24" see-through grid ruler
- sketch book
- pencil and eraser
- Sharpie® ultra fine point marker
- paper scissors
- 3 yards Sulky Totally Stable™. Other foundation material is available but I like this product for its flexibility.

The adventure of this process is now waiting for you. Gather your tools and supplies and begin the journey. This exercise most often results in a small asymmetrical art piece. Give your left brain a rest and stay open to all possibilities.

- The border design should consist of groups of radiating lines; sections of geometric forms (squares or triangles, etc.) and curved lines.
- These lines can be any size and combination that you choose.
- Try extending some of the curved shapes beyond the border edges.
- In your sketchbook do small border free-hand sketches containing all the required design elements. Play with ideas and possibilities.
- When you have a plan that you want to develop, translate the plan on the large paper.
- Place the large sheet of drawing paper on the table.

Drawing the full-size cartoon

- Drawing the outline of the border:
  1) draw a line 6" in from the edge the length of the long side stopping 6" from the edge.
  2) draw a line 6" in from the edge along the short side until it meets the first line.

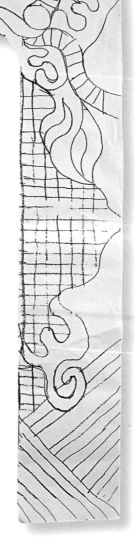

• Draw the radiating lines.

• Freehand the curved design lines on the drawing paper border.

• Draw the geometric forms to fit the 6" wide border, i.e., 2" squares, 3" triangles or a combination of rectangles within the 6" width.

• Darken all lines with a marker.

• Add registration marks and number pieces of the curved sections.

• This is your cartoon and will not be cut up or sewn on.

• Cartoons can be altered at any time by drawing in new lines or layering new template paper on top of the original cartoon and drawing a new section.

Creating the templates

• Lay Sulky Totally Stable™ on cartoon with shiny side up, covering as much of the border cartoon as possible.

• Use a second piece of Sulky Totally Stable™ to cover the remaining border.

• To seam the two pieces of Sulky™ together to form a complete unit, overlap the pieces about 1/4". Lay shiny side down on the ironing board. With the tip of a hot iron press the overlapped area to hold it together.

• Trace the outline of the border and all the lines with the Sharpie® marker. Regular pens will rub off as you work.

A combination of machine appliqué, seamed piecing, and foundation piecing is used to develop the design. This is a very forgiving method of development. The design can be overlaid and changed at any time.

- Pin your cartoon to the design wall.

- sewing machine
- 80/12 embroidery needles
- neutral colored thread
- nylon invisible thread
- scissors
- pins
- rotary cutter, cutting mat, and see-through grid ruler
- fabric:
  a variety of 20 (1/2 yard) pieces coordinating fabrics. Lights, mediums and darks (choose a color palette that appeals to you)

Foundation piecing sewing machine setup

- Reduce stitch length to 2.0 so foundation is perforated for easy removal.
- Regular thread in top and bobbin.
- Run stitch test and adjust tension if necessary.

Foundation piecing the radiating line section

Foundation piecing starts with a paper template that has the design stitching lines drawn on the paper. All the fabric for each section/piece is cut slightly larger than the section. The sequence in which the pieces are sewn together is an important factor and is different with each design. In each case you will determine the sequence before you begin.

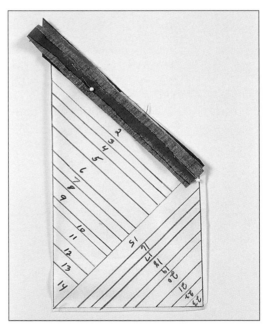

- Cut out a radiating line section from the border template.
- Audition fabric for this radiating line section.

- Pin the pieces of fabric to the wall to determine a pleasing sequence of colors and combination of fabrics.

- Cut strips of fabric at least 1/2" larger than actual section.

- The first fabric piece is placed right side up covering the first section.

- The second piece in the sequence is then placed face down on top of the first piece, making sure both pieces extend a 1/2" seam allowance past the stitching line.

- Make certain the fabric is large enough to cover each section.

- To double check coverage, flip open along the stitching line to make sure the next section is covered.

- Stitching is done from the reverse side and exactly on the drawn line.

- Return to the right side (fabric side up) and trim seam allowance to 1/4".

- The top fabric is then folded open and finger pressed flat with fabric right side up.

- Each fabric in the sequence is added in the same manner until the design is complete. See The Challenge of Spirals chapter for detailed foundation piecing information.

- Pin the completed section in position on the cartoon on the design wall.

- Continue foundation sewing all the radiating sections of your design.

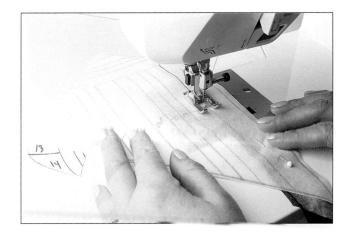

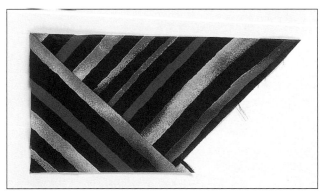

tip

Sometimes you can find the perfect striped fabric to use for the radiating lines instead of foundation piecing them as in the example above.

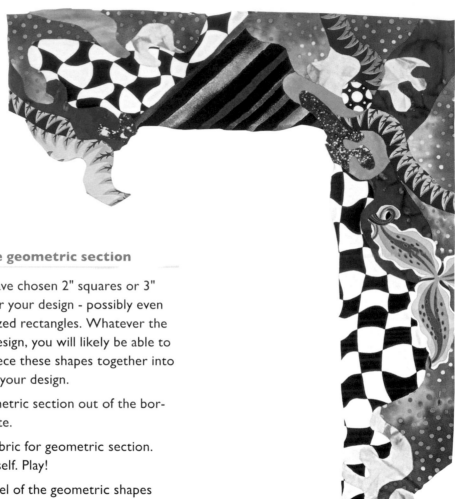

Piecing the geometric section

- You may have chosen 2" squares or 3" triangles for your design - possibly even irregular sized rectangles. Whatever the shape or design, you will likely be able to machine piece these shapes together into a panel for your design.

- Cut a geometric section out of the border template.

- Audition fabric for geometric section. Trust yourself. Play!

- Piece a panel of the geometric shapes that you have chosen that is large enough to cover this geometric section of the design.

- Press the template to the panel and cut out so it has a generous 1/2" seam allowance all the way around the design.

- Pin the section on the cartoon.

tip

Finding a preprinted checkerboard or geometric piece of fabric for your design makes the construction simpler, as in this example.

Machine appliquéing the curved pieces

- Refer to Chapter 7 for instruction on machine appliqué technique for curved pieces.
- Cut a curved section from the border template.
- Audition fabrics as before.
- Develop a complete section, then construct it using machine appliqué.
- Pin in place on the cartoon.

Completing the border

- You must now combine all the different border elements together to form the L-shaped border. This will give your construction and problem solving skills a workout.
- Start at the bottom and build the border up to the corner and then across the top.
- Construction method will depend on which two elements of the border are being added together (see Options).
- Make sure to keep the edges as straight as possible.
- You may straighten these edges a little. Be careful not to cut off any important design element.

options

- A geometric section being joined to a radiating section may be machine pieced.
- If the angle of the radiating section is too sharp, you may wish to machine appliqué the radiating section onto the geometric section.
- The curved section is always machine appliquéd on top of the radiating section or the geometric section.
- If curved shapes extend beyond the border into the interior of the quilt, just leave them hanging. They will be stitched in the final phase of construction.

Have you been able to keep your left brain quiet and allow your right brain to create and play? It is quite a feat to trust and create while not knowing where this design will lead. The border that you have designed and constructed is probably impressive in and of itself, but there is more to come.

The body of the quilt is waiting to be designed. You will want to expand on the border design elements and bring them into the body of the quilt. These elements will probably be enlarged and become the focus of the design. As I said at the start, this is a conversation between the border and the body of the quilt.

options

• The focal point of the design can be in the center with the border design on only two sides creating an asymetrical image.

• The body of the quilt design can be focused in the lower corner to balance the upper asymmetrical border creating an engaging art piece.

• Four borders may be added to completely surround the body of the quilt.

• The central design can be more dramatic and supported by the border or the border can demand as much attention as the center as long as it is an entirely integrated design.

• The border design may continue in the same scale into the center creating a rich textural piece.

Designing the body of the quilt

• With sketchbook in hand observe the completed border.

• Choose some of its design elements or shapes that you would like to develop into a larger scale drawing for the body of the quilt.

• Sketch ideas using some curved shapes from the border design.

• Support this design with a background of geometric shapes and radiating lines.

• Develop the ideas into an interesting composition.

Enlarging the drawing

• Translate your sketch to a full-size cartoon.

• The enlarged drawing should be 20" x 26".

• Freehand draw curved lines and radiating lines on large paper.

Constructing a geometric panel

The central design elements will be supported by a geometric background. The easiest way to create the background is to construct a panel 20" x 26" of the geometric shapes or shapes that are contained in your design, i.e., triangles, squares or rectangles.

• Determine the size of pieces needed.

• Cut out the geometric shapes adding seam allowances.

• Machine piece the entire panel or use a pre-printed geometric fabric.

Finishing construction steps

• Construct the central image using the same techniques as for border.

  1) Position and stitch radiating section to the geometric panel.

  2) Float the curved shapes on top of design and machine appliqué down.

• Additional design elements may be added by machine appliqué or fusing.

Invasion's center was constructed on a pre-printed geometric background.

Invasion, 2004. 26" x 32"

Combining the border and the body

- Machine piece the border or borders to the body.

- Extended shapes:

  Do not catch the shapes when piecing the border on. Leave the overlapping sections loose.

  Machine appliqué the shapes to the body or to the border, wherever the extended shape overlaps the other.

Your unique original piece of art is now ready to be layered, quilted and embellished. This exercise should expand how you think about borders. An integrated image keeps the viewer engaged in the image, while a disjointed image leaves the viewer perplexed and unsatisfied. The opportunity to play with different shapes and design elements was an added bonus. Hopefully images of future designs are dancing in your head!

An integrated image keeps the viewer engaged.

Time Warp, 1999. 84" x 60"

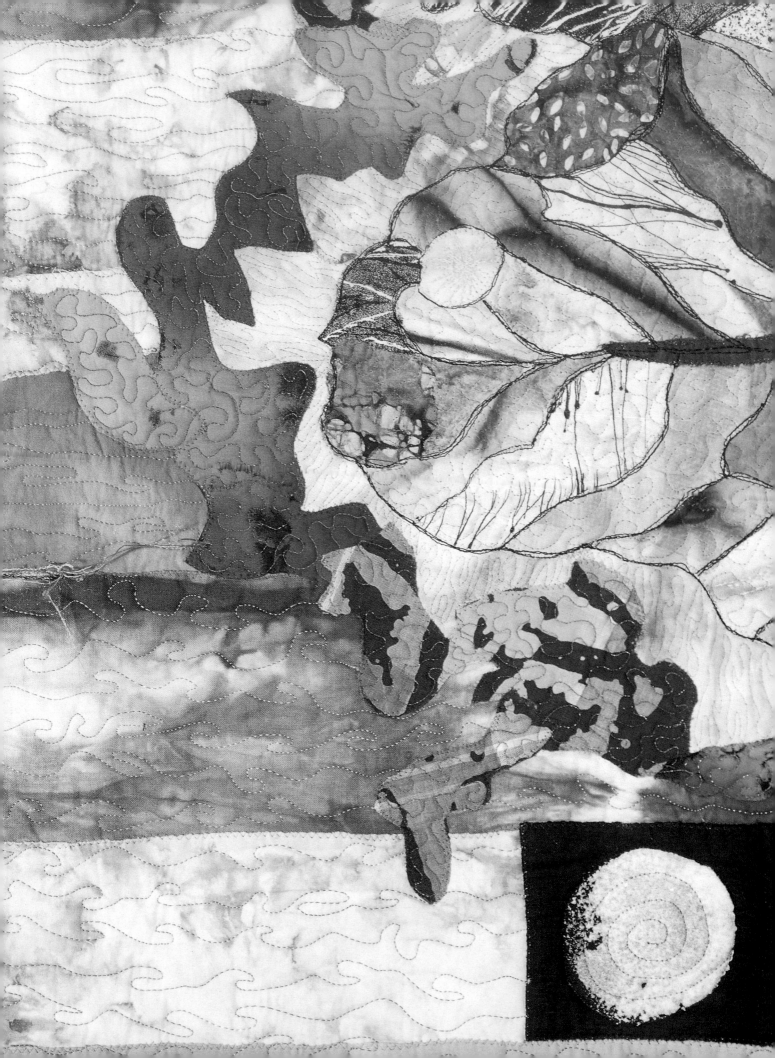

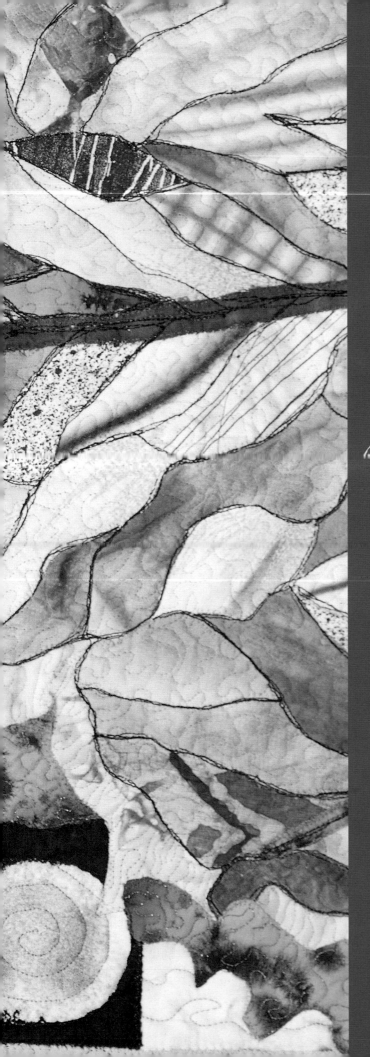

speeding up the process

There are many available construction alternatives to consider when making art quilts with your unique vision. Up to this point, methods such as basic piecing, foundation piecing and turned-edge machine appliqué afforded me the opportunity to construct any image that I chose. Although the processes were time-consuming, they produced the quality of work that I desired. I loved the finished edges that turned-edge machine appliqué achieved. Different artists used other design and construction techniques but they were not for me. Raw edges? Never! Why change what works? Well, never say never. Change often comes to you in unexpected packages.

While doing studio work at a national retreat, I had the good fortune of working in a space adjoining the classroom of David Walker whose work I admire. I was drawn into his space to enjoy his students' work as they progressed. Both students and teacher alike reciprocated the visits. My design and construction process for the quilt *First Thought* varied quite a bit from David's raw edge process. He watched my process with interest as we both design in an intuitive way but he was blown away at the time involved in turning the edges. By the last day he could no longer contain himself. He walked over to the design wall where I was painstakingly turning the edges and whispered "You have got to get a life. Speed up the process. Use fusing, or do some raw edge work," were his words of advice. Most of my pieces have taken six months or more to finish. His words struck a chord; maybe I should consider a process that would allow me to produce more than two quilts a year. I was grateful for his advice.

With my next design *Merlin's Forest,* enlarged and on the wall, I contemplated a new construction process. Fusible webs were unpredictable when I had worked with them years ago. What were the alternatives? I had used a fusible Pellon fleece in a craft project and thought it might work for this new piece. The quilt pieces could be fused directly to the fleece, which would then also serve as the foundation and batting. I would use my same template process, but remove the template and place each piece on the fleece,

First Thought, 1997. 87" × 87"
Collection of Maureen Hendricks, Potomac, MD

butting edges together. The fusing process went beautifully, but there were raw edges that needed to be tamed. A blanket stitch around each piece solved the problem. It slowed down the completion process, but satisfied the designer (me).

I would like to share this technique in the following exercises. It may be just the process you are looking for. It's fun and fast. The design portion of the process is the same, only the construction process is changed. It offers more immediate results. The products and tools used in this exercise are available at most quilt stores and catalogs. The manufacturers continue to develop better quality products to help make fusing easier and more permanent.

Photo by D. Tilton

Merlin's Forest, 1998. 48" x 76"
This quilt was created using the exact method described in this exercise.

- full-size cartoon complete with registration marks and numbers
- fusible batting or fusible fleece at least 6" larger than the drawing
- Sulky Totally Stable™ Amount will depend on the size of your design.
- Sharpie® ultra fine point marker
- small sharp, pointed scissors
- pins
- mini iron (Clover works well.)
- full-size iron and ironing board
- sewing machine (zigzag or blanket stitch)
- invisible thread
- needle: embroidery 80/12
- optional: bobbin thread
- fabric: a variety of fabrics appropriate in color, style, and amount needed for your design

You will need a completed drawing, enlarged and pinned on the design wall. Sulky Totally Stable™ will be used to develop templates as before. This is an evolutionary design process as always, a conversation between you and the image evolving on the wall. Redrafting at any point is an option. The construction technique is fusing using a fusible batting or fleece.

Fusible Fleece:

This is the first product I used. It was fusible on one side only.

+ It had a stable fusible finish.

+ It contained enough fusible finish to adhere the fabric well.

- The fleece stretched.

Fusible Batting:

+ Fusible on both sides, which makes layering the quilt sandwich easier.

+ Stable with little stretching.

+ Lightweight.

+ Comes in many sizes.

- The fusible web sometimes becomes detached and will tear.

Developing your composition in fabric

- Pin the fusible batting cut at least 3" larger than cartoon to design wall.

- Pin the full size cartoon on the design wall next to the batting.

- Determine the center of the batting and of the drawing and mark both.

- Choose an area to start. (This will depend on your creative style, i.e., I always start in the center).

- Pin Sulky Totally Stable™ on the drawing (shiny side toward you) over the area that you have chosen and trace.

- As before, do not trace all the templates for the entire piece before you start. This will allow you the option to edit later.

- With a Sharpie® completely trace the lines, registration marks and numbers that the template material covers.

- Place traced template material on your table.

- Cut out the first template piece of your choice, exactly on the line.

- Cut only the template you intend to work with. Too many precut pieces become easily misplaced.

- Audition fabrics.

- Lightly press the template onto the back of the chosen fabric.

- Cut around the template exactly – no seam allowance.

- Remove the template.

- Pin onto the fleece in approximately the same position as it goes in the cartoon.

- If the fabric does not work as you had expected, just reuse the template and press on to a new fabric choice. Templates can be reused many times.

- Continue the process for each template piece until the first section you chose to work on is completed.

- Once you are happy with a section, while still on the wall, lightly iron pieces onto batting with a mini iron, making sure all the edges are touching each other and no batting shows through.

- Begin the next section by placing template material over a section adjoining the completed section and trace. See p. 66 for instructions.

- Borders can also be fused onto fleece.

- When entire design is completed, use a mini iron and lightly press on the batting. Next take the batting to the ironing board and press securely with a regular iron.

Stitching raw edges

- Use invisible thread in the top and light-weight bobbin thread in the bobbin.
- Use a blanket or zigzag stitch.
- Stitch around each piece to secure raw edges.
- The piece is ready to be layered.

  If using double-sided fusible batting, fuse backing fabric to the other side.

  Pin basting or basting spray can be used to secure the quilt layers if necessary.

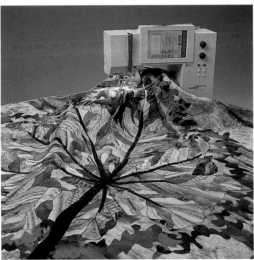

- Quilt as desired.
- Trim away all the fleece that extends beyond the design.
- Straighten edges.
- Bind the quilt.

 tips

- Placing the drawing on the design wall provides a constant visual reference for accurate placement of pieces on the batting.
- You can measure the position on the drawing and translate the measurements to the batting for your first pieces. Everything will build on those first pieces.
- Be sure the iron does not touch the fusible webbing on batting directly or it will melt the adhesive onto the iron.
- If the design wants to change, use techniques learned in Chapter 8 to redraft your design.

creating with fusible batting

Fusible fleece, or batting, works well to collage a quilt or a background. It is fun to compose with different shapes or strips right on the fleece wall. An amazing tapestry can be created. Don't worry if all the fabric does not come in contact with the fusible surface; because of overlap it will be fully attached in the quilting process. When you are happy with the composition just fuse the fabric to the fleece with your mini iron. You now have a background to support a central design of your choice or this may create a quilt top in and of itself ready to be layered and embellished.

A design to be imposed on a fused background can be fused with a fusible web or machine appliquéd onto the background.

These pieces can tend to be a little stiff and one-dimensional so it enhances the design if you add texture. Decorative stitching and yarns can add textural interest to a fused piece. The quilting adds another dimension.

When you need to get a piece done in a short time frame, this is a great technique. I now switch back and forth between fusing and machine appliqué. It depends on what I am trying to achieve as to which process I choose. Sometimes a combination of all the techniques is needed. The larger the tool chest of techniques that you have to draw upon, the more opportunity you will have to express your unique vision.

Phases: Forest Tapestry, 1997. 46" x 46"

Collection of Linda Teufel, Worthington, OH

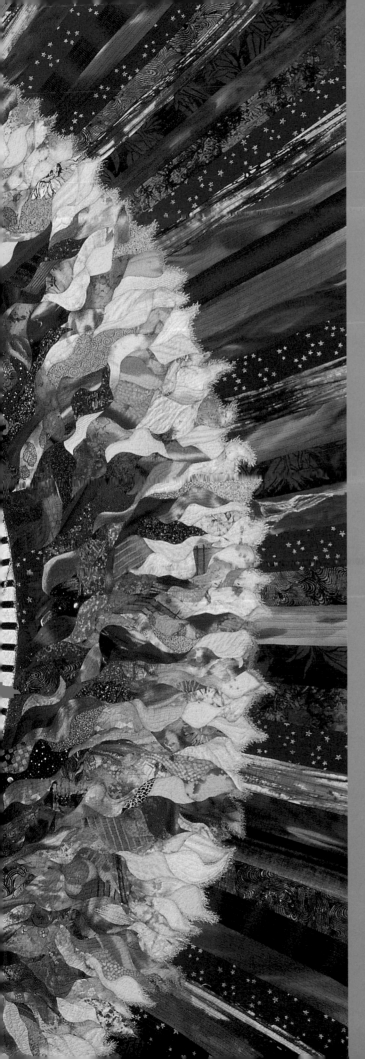

mystical castles

Castles images stir my creative juices, but doing another castle piece was put on hold after creating *City of the Midnight Sun* using turned-edge machine appliqué. The process was cumbersome and time consuming. Turning the edges of all the tiny pieces needed to develop the castles was difficult. I liked the time-saving fusing process as used in the previous chapter so, what if, I created a castle using a stained-glass fusing technique and obtained a new, very dramatic effect? *Atlantis: An Ancient Message* was the outcome of using the new stained-glass fusing technique. This technique allowed me to play, with more immediate results. Mystical castles also fit my innate design style well (to begin in the center and to build on that central image). My preference for bright, bold colors partnered with black and white are also present in my versions of mystical castles. New in my process was fusing to a black background to obtain a stained glass effect.

City of the Midnight Sun, 1996. 101" x 101"

purples, greens and yellows. Doorways peeked out of the nooks and crannies. Strips, novelty prints and batiks brought the castle to life. This was to be a small wall hanging but, as the design developed, it grew to 101" square. The stairway became black and white instead of a yellow brick road. Water and a flaming sky surrounded the castle. To finalize the design, a deep space strata was added. Responding and playing brought my original vision into being, but with a whole new energy—*City of the Midnight Sun.* Using turned-edge machine appliqué was the only hard part of this process.

My vision of a castle was the Emerald City from *The Wizard of Oz.* On a rainy camping trip I began to draw a castle. A large piece of paper, a pencil, an eraser and a ruler were my only tools. No reference pictures were available—just my imagination. Consequently, nothing about the drawing was architecturally correct, but I thought it looked good. Back in the studio I began adding fabric—green fabric—but from the very first piece it did not want to be all green. The castle became a bright colorful image gradating from reds to blues,

quilt. The checkerboard killed the energy of the castle. So what *did* it want? A dimensional cloud, upon which the castle floats, supports and enhances the energy of the castle. Using the stained-glass technique gave each piece prominence and speeded up the construction process. The result was *Atlantis: An Ancient Message*. This piece won the Vision of Tomorrow category of IQA's 2000 Millennium contest.

Atlantis: An Ancient Message evolved in much the same manner. I began this drawing in a remote fishing lodge in northern Alaska. Getting my brain out of the way and isolation seemed to be the best environment for the castle drawings to manifest. As with the previous quilt, this new castle took on a direction of its own right away. My original intent was to set this castle on a deep space checkerboard. "No way," was the response I received from the

Atlantis: An Ancient Message, 2000. 78" X 78"
Collection of Karey Bresenhan, Quilts Inc., Houston, TX

What is your vision for a castle quilt? Is it a childhood version of Cinderella and her prince dancing at the castle ball? Maybe it is the Emerald City as portrayed in *The Wizard of Oz*. Could it be a castle set in the foggy moors of Ireland? One or both of the exercises below are your opportunity to play and bring your vision to life in fabric.

As you begin the design process, leave your ideas of an architecturally accurate building behind. Our castles are going to be wondrous creations straight out of fantasyland. Lines may or may not be straight. Proportions may be exaggerated. The colors can be bright and playful. You can pull from your fabric collection of novelty prints—stripes, checks, batiks—just to name a few. The individual pieces will be mounted to reveal a black background creating a stained-glass effect. There is nothing left to do now but play!

Start your creative juices by looking at some of the possibilities. Let these words or ideas engage your imagination. One may trigger a memory or a different idea. There are no limits.

Coloring books and children's books are excellent resources for castle drawings. Check your local library for books containing castles. The castle scenes can easily be constructed with the stained glass fusing technique.

possibilities & ideas

- The Emerald City in *The Wizard of Oz*
- Cinderella or Sleeping Beauty's castles
- A castle among the clouds
- An ice castle created from crystal shapes
- A planetary vision: sun, moon, stars, planets and castles
- A religious scene: churches, missions or temples
- Monasteries built on cliffs or high mountain peaks
- An ancient tropical temple over-grown with foliage
- Fortresses, including towers, moats and draw-bridges
- Castles set against the moors and fields of Ireland
- A vampire's castle shrouded in the fog
- A castle rising up out of a lake dripping with water and moss
- Native American cliff dwellings or teepee villages
- A hillside of villas in the Greek isles set against blue water
- The skyline of a large city
- An inner-city housing project
- A street lined with shops

Replicating a castle drawing

This drawing, *Sun Castle*, can be enlarged and used as is or the image may be used as a base for your own creative ideas. Maybe a different background. Possibly alter the towers and building to convey a theme (see sketches p. 124).

- Start with the Sun Castle drawing or your version of this Sun Castle.

- Enlarge this drawing 480% on a photocopy machine that has a 36" wide capability. 24" x 24" is a nice workable size.

- Number each piece. Registration marks are not necessary to assemble this piece.

For a 24" block:

- access to a copy machine that enlarges to 36" or a large sheet of paper to draft the design. (See page 50 for enlarging options.)

- small sharp, pointed scissors

- pins

- 1½ yards fusible web (purchased by the yard or in packages)

- black fabric at least 6" larger than your drawing (i.e., 24" x 24" drawing – 30" x 30" black fabric)

- a variety of fabrics in the colors and values that you would like to use

- optional: mini iron (Clover works well.)

- optional: invisible nylon thread for securing the edges

materials and supplies

Positioning pieces

Start with the center pieces when positioning the template pieces on the black fabric. Some distortion may happen. You will be judging the correct position by eye. There is no drawing on the black fabric. Don't worry. This is an improvisational design.

Chose fabrics that add shading and depth. Play and use unexpected fabric and color combinations.

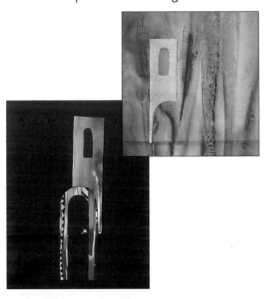

- After tracing, pin the drawing on the wall, fusible web attached, next to the black fabric for reference.

- All templates are cut slightly smaller to obtain a space between the pieces for the stained-glass effect.

- Starting in the center, cut the first template piece slightly smaller than the template.

- Hand press the template to the reverse side of the chosen fabric.

- Cut out with no seam allowance.

- Position this piece on the black fabric in the approximate place of the design.

- Continue cutting out one template at a time, hand pressing it to the back of the fabric, cutting it out, and positioning it on the wall.

- Evaluate the design as it grows and make sure that there is a gap between the pieces that reveals the black underneath. You may need to trim the pieces to achieve the desired black outlines.

Pressing

When the entire castle design is in place on the black fabric, press lightly while still on the wall. Use a small hand held mini iron to do this. If none is available, empty water out of your regular iron, turn off steam setting, take the iron to the wall and lightly press. If you have to remove the design from the wall before pressing, pin pieces in place so as not to misplace or move pieces.

• Press each piece into place, starting in the center, adjusting positioning if necessary

• Remove the entire pressed piece from the wall and press at ironing board according to manufacturer's directions.

tip Using an appliqué pressing cloth is recommended, which may require a few more seconds of heat to secure the pieces.

options

• Use invisible or decorative thread to stitch around each piece with a blanket stitch or zigzag stitch to finish the edges.

• Leave raw edges, layer and quilt.

• Embellish as desired using decorative stitching, couched yarns or beads.

• Quilt the castle with the same responsive openness as when designing the castle.

Sun Castle, 2001. 28" x 28"

Designing a mystical castle

This is your opportunity to design a unique castle scene. Use your resource materials or vision to decide what scene you would like to portray. It helps to keep lines to a minimum. Mountains, water or other shapes should be kept simple for this exercise. Save the more complex images for a future quilt. Remember the fabrics can create much of the depth and shading for you.

materials and supplies

- resource or inspirational materials
- sketch book
- pencil and eraser
- tracing paper
- Sharpie® fine-point marker
- access to a copy machine that enlarges to 36" or a large sheet of paper to draft your design. (See page 50 for enlarging options.)

- Sketch different castles in different settings in your sketch book.
- Choose a castle drawing that you would like to develop.
- Trace the small castle drawing.
- Castle lines may be exaggerated or bent as you trace.
- Replicate the background lines from your sketchbook drawing around this castle.
- Play and improvise, respond to the drawing as it develops.
- Work on the image until you have a good composition.
- Darken all lines with a Sharpie® marker.
- Number each piece. Registration marks are not necessary to assemble this piece.
- Enlarge the drawing to the desired size.
- Continue designing and construction as in exercise Replicating a Castle Drawing.

Questions to ask yourself:

- Did your image evolve as you anticipated?
- How can you use this technique in future quilts?
- What possibilities have these playful exercises evoked?

Hopefully, the playful attitude used in these castles will continue to be prevalent in all your creative work.

We Are Not In Kansas Anymore, 66" x 66", by Karlyn Lohrenz, Billings, MT

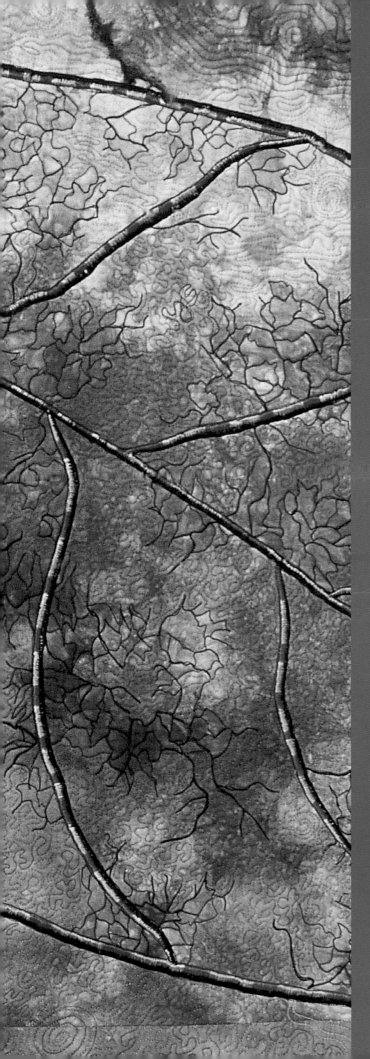

nature's language

Here is another *what if?* What if I pulled out the most prized, luscious, hand-dyed, and hand-painted fabrics and used them? You know the fabrics I'm talking about—the pieces that spoke to you, the fabrics that you first walked away from, but were then drawn back to. Leaving without purchasing them was not an option. You always intended to use these majestic fabrics, but when it comes time to cut them, you just can't do it. These pieces are too wonderful to touch with a rotary cutter or scissors. The images, the texture, and the lines are a piece of art in and of themselves. Often these fabrics live on your design wall for a time and inspire possible design scenarios. Then they usually get fondled, folded, and placed back in the stash with a gentle pat, but never used. Now you know how crazy and loving I can be about pieces of fabric, but I will bet most of you can relate to this experience.

The question always in the back of my mind was how could I do these fabrics justice? The answer came one day when one of these special fabrics was taking its turn living on the design wall. As I walked into the studio and glanced at the fabric, there was an amazing leaf image displayed across the surface. The light bulb went on! What if I just used stitching to bring out the image? What if the piece was about the texture in the fabric? So the challenge was set; I was willing to begin. The piece would take me on a new evolutionary journey. I urge you to take this journey with some of your prized fabrics. This is an experience of responding to the image and building texture with threads and yarns.

materials and supplies

- sewing machine (feed dogs must retract, must have zigzag stitch)
- feet: open-toed and darning feet
- rotary cutter, mat and ruler
- scissors
- marking tool: light and dark fabric marking tools
- stabilizer: Sulky Totally Stable™ (same size as fabric)
- thread: a variety of decorative threads
- optional: decorative yarns
- lingerie bobbin thread
- 1¼ yards fusible batting. See page 112.
- optional: regular batting of your choice and adhesive basting spray
- Fabric: one piece of hand-dyed or painted fabric. It is easier to use one yard or smaller pieces. Try several different pieces before settling on one to develop. (See resource guide for hand-dyed fabric sources.)
- 1¼ yard backing fabric

Developing the design

Audition several pieces of your unique, textural fabrics on the design wall. Take only a minute or two to consider the fabrics. Do not overthink this part because you will intuitively pick the best one to work on.

- Place the fabric of your choice in the middle of your design wall.

- Close your eyes, take a few deep breaths and center yourself.

- Relax and respond to images in the fabric.

- Feel what is there? (The slowest way to create is thinking.)

- Feel the emotions it evokes?

- Descriptive words can help stimulate your imagination. Use my list as a resource and add to the list or jot down words in your sketchbook when developing designs.

- Where is the focus? Where does the eye lead?

- Doodle some design possibilities in your sketchbook.

- Choose a large design element that will be your major focus.

- This large design element will be executed in a bold satin stitch.

descriptive words	
peaceful	chaotic
subtle	powerful
spiraling	evolving
flowing	expanding
weaving	grids
implied	engaging
beginning	ending
light	dark
exploding	shadows
majestic	awesome
organic	symbolic
simple	Iridescent
music	wispy

Detail from **Kiss of the Creative Fire**

Marking Design on Fabric

- Stabilize fabric: press Sulky Totally Stable™ shiny side down onto the back of fabric.

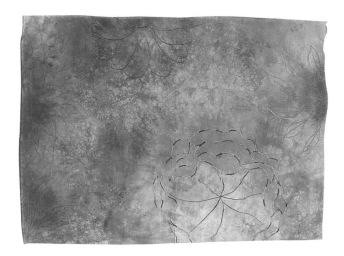

- Mark predominate design only on the fabric.
  for dark fabric: silver pencil or chalk
  for light fabric: drawing pencil (can be erased with gum eraser) or fade away marking pencil.

Stitching Major Design Elements

Set the stage for your thread composition by using a satin stitch to outline your major design element. Dark or contrasting thread helps highlight the lines. Variegated colored thread adds an interesting textural effect. A second row of stitching can be added to make a bold statement.

sewing machine set-up

- Open-toed embroidery or machine recommended foot for the satin stitch.
- Bobbin: regular or lingerie bobbin thread (Lingerie thread does not build up as much on the back when doing heavy stitching.)
- Embroidery thread in top To avoid skipped stitches match top and bobbin threads. If synthetic thread is used on top, using cotton in the bobbin may cause skipped stitches.
- Embroidery or Metafil needle will give you a more even satin stitch.
- Zigzag stitch; adjust for wide satin stitch.
- Run test stitches on scraps of fabric, adjust setting until you have a good stitch.
- Adjust top and bobbin tension if necessary.
- Record information in your sketchbook or store in machine's program. (Each machine will be different.)

tip

The sharper the needle the easier it is to produce a nice even satin stitch.

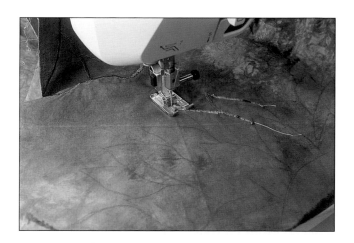

- Stitch design outline, moving slowly to achieve a smooth filled-in satin stitch.

- A second row of the same color or a contrasting color can be added to enhance lines.

- Couching decorative threads or yarns along satin stitch can also create bolder lines.

- Clip threads and remove Sulky™ from back after all your satin stitching or couching is completed.

option

Free-motion zig zag stitch. Feed dogs dropped and stitch thickness controlled by hand. (Recommended resource: *Quilting Arts*, Issue 7—Ellen Anne Eddy, p. 28)

Developing the composition

The design lines that you have developed on the surface of the fabric may not be strong enough to create an interesting composition. Additional design elements may need to be added. The size, shape and placement of these elements should support, but not overpower, the fabric and the stitched texture. Remember, this is about responding to the fabric and keeping the image simple. The final design component is the addition of quilted texture after the composition is layered.

options for additional design elements

- These new design elements should focus the eye and keep the viewer engaged in the composition.
- You may need a subtle texture or color change in selected areas.
- A bold shape or additional fabric may be needed to balance an off-center image.
- Unexpected fun or whimsical fabric can add interest.
- The new shapes may be used to create an asymmetrical design.
- Possibly only a border is needed to highlight the design.
- An irregular outside edge may add interest.

Adding fabric design elements

For this exercise limit the amount of additional design elements to five.

- Sketch some ideas before auditioning fabric for these elements.
- Free form fabric cutting without templates is a simple technique for this exercise.
- Templates may be needed if the design element is an intricate shape.
- Compose on the wall and stay open to design opportunities as they present themselves.
- Audition different fabrics for color and placement on surface of top.
- Free hand cut out the shapes or strips.
- Audition these cut pieces on the wall for correct proportion.
- Play; move the pieces around until you have an engaging and balanced composition.
- Turn the entire piece on its side for a different prospective.

tip

Consider the possibility of reducing the size of the original fabric if the composition feels empty or incomplete.

Applying the fabric pieces

- Use machine piecing for any border pieces.
- Fusing the shapes is the simplest construction process for this project.
- Machine appliqué and templates are other alternatives to consider.

Once all the additional fabric pieces are applied to your top, press and straighten edges (unless the design calls for irregular edges).

Layering the quilt

Quilts may be layered in many different ways. I prefer fusible batting for a small project. Pin basting can be cumbersome when quilting heavy texture on a small piece. Hobbs Wool batting and pin basting every 6" is my choice for a larger piece.

- Cut backing and batting at least 4" larger than the finished top.
- First fuse the top onto fusible batting according to manufacturer's instructions.
- Then fuse the backing fabric to the back of the batting.
- Optional: Use regular batting and adhesive basting spray to layer the quilt.

tip

Fusing the layers together is better than pin basting when developing heavy texture and quilted veins. Pin removal interferes with a good stitching rhythm on a small piece.

Messengers, 1998. 36" x 48"
Collection of Susan Heidiecooper, Wilson, WY

As the design evolves, respond to the new design possibilities.

Adding texture & quilting

Place the layered piece back on the design wall. Sit comfortably facing your composition, take a few deep breaths, close your eyes and center yourself. Sit with the piece and develop a tentative quilting design plan. Respond to the surface and let the lines or images on the fabric lead you. If necessary, mark some of the lines on the fabric. It is easiest to use free-motion quilting lines to enhance design. Use a variety of colors and types of threads when developing the texture. I may use as many as 20 different threads on the top and in the bobbin when quilting a piece.

sewing machine set-up

- drop feed dogs
- darning foot
- needle—depends on thread and fabric.
- bobbin thread
- decorative thread
- Adjust tensions and run test strips for each new thread if necessary. (Bobbin thread should not be pulled through to the top.)

- Breathe and play with threadwork and surface embellishment.
- Get your whole body involved in the rhythm. Feel the motion of the piece and quilt those lines with your machine.

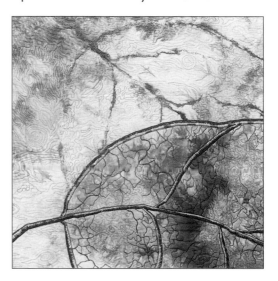

- More yarns or beads can be added by couching them to surface for an added design element.
- The finished quilt may need to be blocked before binding.

This is a fun and fast process. It gives you the opportunity to learn and play with building texture in a piece. These techniques will translate into your future pieces. You will look at fabric with a new perspective. Creating your own fabric is an inviting proposition. The possibilities are endless when responding to the surface of beautiful, original pieces of fabric.

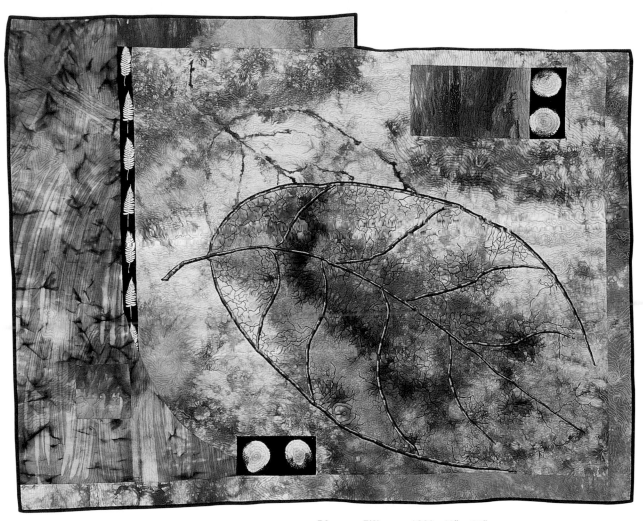

Phases: Filigree, 1999. 40" x 51"
Collection of Carol Beck and Dionne Hersh, Matthies, WA

CHAPTER FIFTEEN

a universe of possibilities

Just Breathe exemplifies many of the possibilities I saw for myself at this time in my life. This piece is filled with my joy. Energy abounds in each and every flower. The water is alive with movement and depth. The butterfly's whimsical nature is evident for the entire world to see. I loved making every single petal, flower, leaf, butterfly, water ripple, and rock. Every day when I walked into the studio as this image evolved on the wall, I was bursting with excitement and anticipation. Each stitch added more marvelous texture. I could almost smell the flowers in this imaginary garden. The riot of color feeds my soul. This is a quilt filled with my spirit and energy.

Though I may sound overly enthusiastic about my work, I have not lost my mind! This is just how much I love what I do. "Thankful" is not a strong enough word for how I feel about the gift I have been given; the gift we all have been given—of being able to manifest our joy in some form.

I realize that not everyone sees what I see in my pieces, nor will everyone like my art. However, I hope that everyone will feel the joy with which it is created. I am sure fault can be found with many elements of my designs. That is okay. What counts is what I learned in the process and that I gave voice to my unique creativity. My hope is that everyone experiences such pleasure when they are creating. This is what we are all striving for—doing what we love and loving what we do.

From these possibilities all other possibilities have sprung.

When I began this journey into the realm of quilting, I did not even imagine the world of possibilities it held for me. Below are some of the most notable steps in my journey. These are the things that make me believe there is a purpose to the universe and that I was drawn to create quilts for a reason:

- First and foremost: the gift of creating the quilts and being part of the quilting community.

- My development from copying traditional quilt patterns to creating art quilts.

- *In The Beginning* being chosen as one of the top 100 American quilts of the century is amazing. The quilt was made for the joy of creating it, not with the intent of winning an award.

- The surprise of discovering that other people respond to my work and that work being chosen to receive many awards.

- The opportunity to teach what I know, nationally and internationally. I happily embrace this opportunity to inspire the creative impulse in others.

- The opportunity to lecture about understanding creativity and to tell my story is an amazing development.

- One of the most astonishing opportunities is writing this book. To be able to help free the creative spirit in others and to guide them in manifesting their unique creative visions is an awesome gift.

Just Breathe, 2002. 70" x 86"

Writing a book is alien to a visual person like me with a mediocre usage of the English language. But the universe has seen fit to give me this task and I have worked hard to impart the knowledge I have. It also helped to have a wonderful friend who gave generously of her time to edit my work. To have a wonderful publisher who believed in my vision for this book made the process enjoyable. By the way, I had to pin the written pages up on the design wall to see how the information was flowing. It's weird, but it worked for me.

In this book, I have shared some of what has resulted from my belief in an endless well of possibilities that the universe has to offer. It is my hope that you will see the possibilities that the world of unique expression offers you. Twenty years ago, these things never would have been possible for me. Quilting revealed the innate gifts I came into this world with. Believe me, they were well hidden! Are your gifts being used or are they buried under a mountain of rules and self-doubt? Trust in your abilities and create what you love. Who knows what exciting possibilities will present themselves to you.

"Imagination is more important than knowledge!"

— Albert Einstein

I hope this book has touched your life in a positive way. A willing spirit and a desire to create open the door into the world of your unique creative expression. When I opened the door into the realm of art quilting, I had no concept of the power this action would hold. It is often the small unassuming actions we take that have the most impact on our lives. Do not discount the wondrous images you create; they have great power. They have the power to catapult you into whole new levels of self-expression and opportunity.

Maybe you chose the extraordinary path of exploring this book from beginning to end. Did you try each exercise as you went? Perhaps one or more of the techniques struck a chord and launched you into beginning the development of a unique body of work. Was it your objective to create more innovative quilts or develop a personal style when you picked up this book? Possibly your ideas and concepts were in place and all you needed was a construction technique from this book to bring your ideas to life. Maybe you are an artist learning to use fabric as your new medium. Whatever your reason for reading and using this book, I sincerely hope that your expectations were fulfilled.

It is my hope that you will see the possibilities that the world of unique expression offers you and that you will continue the journey of creating and presenting your joy to the world. Your unique creative vision unfolds with every breath. Celebrate and trust your imagination.

Prismatic Flowers, 2004. 71" x 71"

resources

Bernina
3702 Prairie Lake Ct.
Aurora, IL 60504
800-877-0477
www.berninausa.com

Baby Lock
1760 Gilsinn Lane
Fenton, MO 63026
800-482-2669
www.babylock.com

Bali Fabrics
21787 8th St. East #1
Sonoma, CA 95476
707-996-1445
www.balifab.com

Clover
1007 E. Dominguez St.
Carson, CA 90746
800-233-1703
www.clover-usa.com

Dragon Threads
490 Tucker Dr.
Worthington, OH 43085
614-841-9388
www.dragonthreads.com

Elna
1760 Gilsinn Lane
Fenton, MO 63026
800-848-elna
www.elnausa.com

Fairfield Processing
batting
88 Rose Hill Ave
Danbury, CT 06810
800-980-8000
www.fairfield.com

Fiskars
Scissors, rotary cutter, mats
Box 8027
Wausau, WI 54402
800-950-0203
www.fiskars.com

Free Spirit Fabrics
1350 Broadway
NY, NY 10018
212-279-0888
www.freespiritfabric.com

Heritage Cutlery
7971 Refinery Rd
Bolivar, NY 14715
800-252-8452
www.heritagecutlery.com

Hobbs Bonded Fibers
batting
Box 2521
Waco, TX 76702
254-741-0040
www.hobbsbondedfibers.com

Hoffman California Fabrics
25792 Obrero Dr.
Mission Viejo, CA 92691
949-770-2922

Janome of America
10 Industrial Ave.
Mahwah, NJ 07430
201-825-3200
www.janome.com

Koala Cabinets
Madeira Threads
Klassé Scissors
9631 N.E. Colfax St
Portland, OR 97220
503-858-1452

Nancy's Notions
333 Beichl Ave.
Beaver Dam, WI 53918
www.nancysnotions.com

Barbara Olson
20 Emerald Hills Dr.
Billings, MT 59101
www.barbaraolsonquiltart.com
406-259-2304

Pfaff America
31000 Viking Parkway
Westlake, OH 44145
440-808-6550
www.pfaffusa.com

Robison Anton Threads
Box 159
Fairview, NJ 07022
201-941-0500
www.robisonanton.com

Rowenta
irons
196 Boston Av.
Medford, MA
781-396-0600
www.rowentausa.com

Sulky
3113 Broadpoint Dr.
Harbor Heights, FL 33983
800-874-4115
www.sulky.com

Superior Threads
Box 1672
St. George, UT 84771
800-499-1777
www.superiorthreads.com

The Warm Company
Batting, Steam-A-Seam 2
954 E. Union St.
Seattle, WA 98122
800-234-WARM
www.warmcompany.com

YLI
161 West Main St.
Rock Hill, SC 29730
803-985-3100
www.ylicorp.com

hand-dyed and painted fabrics

Sky Dyes
PO Box 370116
West Hartford, CT 06137-0116
Mickey Lawler
860-232-1429
www.skydyes.com

Laura Wasilowski
324 Vincent Place
Elgin, IL 60123
847-931-7684
www.artfabrik.com

Lunn Fabrics
317 E. Main St.
Lancaster, OH 43130
Michael Mrowka & Debra Lunn
614-654-2202
www.lunnfabrics.com

Just Imagination
PO Box 83
Bow, WA 98232
Judy Robertson
360-766-4030
www.justimagination.com

Fabrics To Dye For
85 Beach St.
Westerly, RI 02891
Jennifer Priestley
888-322-1319
www.fabricstodyefor.com

Art Cloth Studios
Jane Dunnewold
1134 West Agarita Ave.
San Antonio, TX 78201
www.artclothstudios.com

Linda Tilson
1171 Euclid Rd.
Venice, FL 34293
www.ebaystores.com/
id=14181191

Blueberry Farm Designs
Ionne McCauley
705 Corcan Rd.
Qualicum Beach, BC V9K2E9
email: indigo@nanaimo.ark.com

Bold Over Batiks
Mary Scott
458 Warwick St
St Paul, MN 55105
888-830-7455
www.boldoverbatiks.com

suggested reading

The Artist's Way
Julia Cameron

*Drawing On the
Light From Within*
Judith Cornell, PH.D.

Creating Minds
Howard Gardner

Frames of Mind
Howard Gardner

*How to Think Like
Leonardo da Vinci*
Michael J. Gelb

The Creative Artist
Nita Leland

Quilts and Influences
Nancy Crow

Freeing The Creative Spirit
Adriana Diaz

*The Vein of Gold: A Journey to
Your Creative Heart*
Julia Cameron

Handbook of Creativity
Robert Sternberg

Brain Typing
Jonathan P. Niednagel

Threadplay
Libby Lehman

audio tapes

Available through
Nightingale-Conant / 1-800-323-5552
or Sounds True / 1-800-333-9185

Freedom Through Higher Awareness
Dr. Wayne Dyer

The Sacred Journey
Sam Keen

Mind Mapping
Michael Gelb

True Balance
Sonia Choquette

Personal Power
Anthony Robbins

biography

Photo by D. Tilton

Barbara Olson is a national and international award-winning quilt artist, teacher and lecturer. Her quilts have appeared in many publications and exhibits around the world. *In The Beginning,* one of Barbara's art quilts, was chosen as one of *The Twentieth Century's Best American Quilts.* Many of her art quilts are included in private and corporate collections across the country.

For the last ten years she has been developing and giving workshops and lectures for those interested in expanding their unique creative talents in the area of quilt arts. When Barbara is not on the road teaching or judging quilt shows she is at home in her mountain top studio with her husband, two dogs and two cats in Billings, Montana.

Featured Quilts: Books

In The Beginning. p. 69
American Quiltmaking 1970-2000, AQS 2004

Planned Serendipity. p. 33
Hire, Diane. *Oxymorons: Absurdly Logical Quilts.* AQS 2001

Time Warp. July.
Quilt Art Engagement Calendar 2002, AQS

Day One.
"Deep Space Checkerboards." p. 62
Innovative Piecing, Rodale Successful Quilting Library

In The Beginning. p. 47
The Twentieth Century's Best American Quilts: Celebrating 100 Years of the Art of Quiltmaking. Austin, Mary. Primedia 1999

In The Beginning. 53
The Quilt: Beauty in Fabrics and Thread, Salazar, Marie. Michael Friedman Publishing 1997

Village Sunrise. p. 36
Nature's Patterns, Becker, Joyce. Quilt Digest 1996

Featured Quilts: Magazines

Eight selected quilts. cover, pp.13-18
Popular Patchwork, Aug. 2003

Just Breathe. p.40
American Quilter, Fall 2002

Atlantis. p.4
IQA Journal, Winter 2001

Atlantis. p.57
My Patchwork Quilt; Kobe, Japan 2001

Atlantis. back cover
Quilters Newsletter, May 2001

Merlin's Forest. p. 45
American Quilters Society, July 1999

First Thought. p.38
American Quilters Society, July 1998

Four selected quilts.
IQA Journal, Fall 1998 - Interview

City of the Midnight Sun. front cover.
"Designing Outside The Lines"
American Quilters Society, Spring 2000

City of the Midnight Sun. p. 45
Quilters Newsletter, Leman Publications, May 1998

In The Beginning. p.63
Quilters Newsletter, Leman Publications, May 1998

In The Beginning.
Montana Magazine, Lee Enterprises, November 1996

In The Beginning. back cover
Quilters Newsletter, Leman Publications, October 1995 No. 276

Village Sunrise. p.26
Popular Patchwork, Nexus Publications, Vol. 3 No. 5, United Kingdom, Jan./Feb. 1996

Village Sunrise. cover, p.18
Quilts A World Of Beauty, Journal of the American International Quilt Association, Spring 1995

Village Sunrise. p.32
Quilters Newsletter, Leman Publications, April 1995 No. 271

Miracle Windows. pp.48–49
Patchwork Quilts, Lopez Pub. Jan. 1993

Southwest Images. p.34
Patchwork Quilts, Lopez Pub. Sept. 1993

Commissions

Cradle of Peace
Ft. Belnap Senior Citizen Community Center, 1994

Southwest Images
L.A. Olson & Assoc. Inc., Larry Olson P.E., 1991

Mesa Grande
Yellowstone Office Center, Sally Kindsfather, 1990

Collections

Kiss of The Creative Fire
Sally Davey, New Pieces Gallery, Berkley, CA, 2002

Atlantis An Ancient Message
Quilts Inc. Karey Bresenhan, Houston, TX, 2002

Merlin's Forest
Private NC Collection, 2001

Messengers From The Other Side
The Huidekopper Collection, Jackson, WY, 1999

First Thought
The Hendricks Collection, Potomac, MD, 1998

Vibrations of Spirit
Robert & Marjory Taylor, Billings, MT, 1998

Village Sunrise
Private collection, NJ, 1997

In The Beginning
Quilts Incorporated; Karey Bresenhan, Houston, TX, 1997

Day One
Elizabeth Ridgeway M.D., Jackson, WY, 1996

Phases: Forest Tapestry
Linda Teufel, Columbus, OH, 1997

prize-winning quilts

The Alchemist: Stirring The Elements
International Quilt Festival 2002
Second Place / Large Art

Just Breathe
American Quilters Society Show 2002
Second Place / Professional Appliqué

Atlantis: An Ancient Message
International Millennium 2000 Show
First Place / Visions of Tomorrow

Time Warp
Pennsylvania National Quilt Extravaganza 2000
First Place / Innovative

Western Heritage Show 2000
Best of Show

American Quilters Society Show 2000
Honorable Mention

Kiss of the Creative Fire
Quilting In The Tetons 1999
Best Use of Color

Merlin's Forest
Pennsylvania National Quilt Extravaganza 1999
Honorable Mention

American Quilters Society Show 1999
Third Place Wall Quilt, Professional

Phases: Forest Tapestry
Pacific International Quilt Festival 1998
Judges' Choice

Western Heritage Show, Billings, MT 1998
First Place & Best Innovative Design

First Thought
Pennsylvania National Quilt Extravaganza 1998
Best of Show

Great Pacific Northwest Quilt Show 1998
Second Place / Art Quilt

American Quilters Society Show, Paducah, KY 1998
First Place / Innovative Professional

City of the Midnight Sun
Pacific International Quilt Festival,
San Francisco, CA 1997
Best of Show

Great Pacific Northwest Quilt Show,
Seattle, WA 1996
Second Place / Art Mixed

Genesis Revisited
Quilting In The Tetons 1998
Best Surface Design

International Quilt Festival, Houston, TX 1997
Second Place / Large Art

Big Sky Quilt Retreat, Billings, MT 1997
First Place / Viewers' Choice

Day One
Western Heritage Center, Billings, MT 1996
Innovative Design & Third Place Art Quilt

Quilting In The Tetons, Jackson, WY 1996
Surface Design & First Place Art Quilt

Pennsylvania National Quilt Extravaganza 1995
Honorable Mention / Innovative Art

Pacific International Quilt Festival 1995
Honorable Mention / Best Use of Color,
Innovative

In The Beginning
100 American Best Quilts of the Century 2000

International Quilt Association (IQA) 1995
Award of Excellence / Art Quilt, Small

Western Heritage Center, Billings, Montana 1994
Second Place / Innovative Design Large Art

Pennsylvania National Quilt Extravaganza 1994
First Place / Professional Art

Pacific International Quilt Festival 1994
Third Place / Professional Art

Miracle Windows
Quilting In The Tetons 1994
First Place / Art Quilt

Western Heritage Center, Billings, Montana 1992
Original Design / Large Art

Village Sunrise
IQA–International Quilt Festival 1994
Judges' Choice

Study in Plaid
Yellowstone Art Exhibition 1989
First Place / Fiberart

First Thought, 1997. 87" x 87"
Collection of Maureen Hendricks, Potomac, MD